Fishes

A Handbook for Anglers

Andreas Janitzki

Photo credits:
Frank Brodrecht: pp. 65 b, 76, 88, 89 t l, 100, 102, 103 b l, 106, 107 t,
112, 113 b l, 122/123, 124, 126/127, 127 t
Herbert Frei: pp. 7 t, 8 t, 10 t, 18/19, 20 t, 21, 23 b, 34, 36 b, 36/37, 38/39, 42/43, 44,
46, 47 t r, 48, 56, 60/61, 62/63, 66, 67 t l, 68/69, 74/75, 78/79
Frank Hecker: pp. 58, 59 t., 64, 85 b., 90, 92/93, 94/95, 98, 99 t l, 110/111, 118/119, 120/121
Ronny Schmitt: pp. 4/5, 11 b., 12, 22 t l, b, 28/29, 31 t, 33 b
Wolfgang Schulte: pp. 84, 86/87, 96, 100/101, 104/105, 108/109, 114/115, 116/117.
All other photographs are from the author's personal archive.

The following abbreviations have been used throughout the book:

DE	Germany	FR	France
ES	Spain	NL	Netherlands
SE	Sweden	PL	Poland

Disclaimer

All possible care has been taken in the making of this book. Nonetheless, no liability can be assumed for the information contained in it. Neither the author nor the translator nor the publisher can be held responsible for damages resulting from information in this book that is not in accordance with the current legal regulations in the Netherlands or Belgium, or for damages that result from the practical information in the book. Fishing without a license is not permitted. For more detailed information contact fishing organizations, the authorities, and/or obtain information from the Internet.

©VEMAG Verlags- und Medien Aktiengesellschaft, Cologne
www.apollo-intermedia.de

Complete production: VEMAG Verlags- und Medien Aktiengesellschaft, Cologne

Contents

Fishes

provides an overview of 57 of the most popular angling fishes found in European waters, both freshwater and saltwater varieties. The coloured information boxes tell you everything from where to find the fish and their most important characteristics to the best bait to use to catch them. Large underwater photos make identification easy. There is more to successful angling than just baiting a fishing rod, so Fishes also looks at each species' feeding and reproductive habits and growth cycle, as well as the best times and places for catching them. The key to successful angling is to study the habits of each particular fish closely!

Common Bream

Other names: Bronze bream
DE: Brachsen, FR: Brème,
ES: Brema, NL: Brasem,
SE: Braxen, PL: Leszcz

Distribution

Common bream can be found from the Caspian Sea and the Ural River to Western Europe. Although they are found all over central Europe, in the British Isles they are only encountered in England and Ireland—they are not found in Wales, the south-west peninsula or northern Scotland. Common bream are also absent from Scandinavia, and occur only occasionally in the Mediterranean region.

Bream should always be landed using a net.

Common bream prefer still or slow-running waters with muddy bottoms, which the fish dig up with their protruding mouths while searching for food. The slow-flowing stretches of lowland rivers where this species of fish likes to live are known as the "bream zone". Of course, common bream are also at home in lakes, where they occur in large numbers, as they do in almost all the waters they inhabit.

Common bream like to live in shoals. They often form large mixed shoals, particularly with the silver bream, and it can be rather difficult for the less experienced observer to tell the two species apart.

The reproductive period for bream begins in May and lasts into July, depending on weather conditions. During the entire period, the male displays a prominent

Common Bream

spawning rash, particularly around the head. The fish congregate in large shoals near the banks, where they engage in rather violent spawning behaviour. Each female lays as many as 300,000 eggs with a diameter of 1 to 1.5 mm. Common bream spawn in several phases and not necessarily in one place. Instead, they move from place to place, often covering long distances—up to several miles—between each spawning phase.

In comparison with their frequent companion the silver bream, common bream not only develop faster, but grow to be almost twice as large. An average specimen is around 30 to 40 cm long and weighs between 500 g and 2.5 kg. Really large common bream may achieve a length of 80 cm and tip the scales at 6 kg.

Common bream can be caught all year round, but bite especially

The float tip rising out of the water signals the bite of a common bream.

Groundbait balls as big as oranges lure the fish.

The best bait

The number one bait for common bream is maggots, but casters (the chrysalis stage of maggots) and all sorts of worms can also be effective. Bread, dough, pieces of potato, small boilies, sweetcorn, peas, pasta and even jelly babies work quite well, too.

At first glance, this wide range of options may make it seem rather hard to choose bait when fishing for bream. So, to begin with, consider using foods that occur naturally in the fishing area.

Common bream are very flexible in their feeding preferences. When young, they tend to stick to plankton. As they grow older they become bottom feeders, eating midge lar vae and mudworms along with small molluscs, snails and crustacea. In waters with only little bottom-dwelling fauna, however, even adult bream will not pass up thick clouds of plankton.

Common Bream

Characteristics

Common bream are deep-bodied fish, much flattened at the sides. The back varies in colouring from very dark brown to black: older specimens have an additional green or gold shimmer. The light-coloured flanks have a silvery, metallic sheen; the belly is whitish. The terminal or slightly downward facing mouth can extend to form a proboscis, and the distance from the front edge of the eye to the point of the snout is longer than the diameter of the eye. Common bream are very slimy, with large scales and dark grey fins; the paired fins are slightly lighter in colour, and both pectoral fins and anal fin are long.

Catches like this are not an everyday occurrence.

As the fish grow older, their colouring becomes more marked.

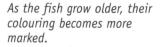

well from April to September. Warm, humid weather and the periods around dawn and dusk have proven to be particularly conducive to good catches. The best angling locations for common bream are those near vegetation growing along the shore and carpets of water lilies.

Bear in mind that ground-baiting is an important ingredient for success when fishing for bream. Sweet groundbait balls enriched with maggots bring the best results. Light legering or float fishing using thin leaders and small hooks should then produce an abundant catch. The bait should be presented on, or close to, the bottom. Note that common bream are very sensitive to noise, so it is advisable to fish from a distance, especially when angling from a boat, when noises cannot be completely avoided. If it is not feasible to remain at a distance from the fishing spot, it is imperative to stay as quiet as possible so as not to disturb the fish or drive them away.

Sturgeon

DE: Stör , FR: Esturgeon,
ES: Esturión, NL: Stent,
stuer, SE: Stör, PL: Jesiotr
zachodni

Distribution

In the Danube system, the sturgeon is only found in the delta. It lives in coastal waters from the North Cape, North Sea, Baltic and northern Mediterranean all the way to the Black Sea, as well as in the lower and middle reaches of the larger rivers. Sturgeon visit Great Britain's waters only rarely.

Except during their reproductive period, sturgeon are found mostly in marine tidal zones. They are anadromous and start leaving their regular habitats around March to travel to their spawning grounds in the lower reaches of rivers. Spawning generally occurs in June and July. However, depending on weather conditions and the distance to be travelled, the spawning period can last into August. The female lays up to 2.5 million eggs, 2 to 3 mm in size, over solid bottoms or gravel banks. The fry take only three to six days to hatch, but the young fish often do not begin to migrate towards the sea until they have reached a length of 40 to 60 cm—when they are between two and four years old. They then often remain for some time in the brackish water at the mouths of rivers, as they cannot endure the salt concentrations found in the open sea until they reach the age of four or five. Adult sturgeon are 1 to 2 m long on average, with males remaining smaller than females. Very old specimens can reach a length of up to 6 m and a weight of 1,000 kg, but these days such magnificent sturgeon are a great rarity.

Heavy legering or float fishing are best when you are going after sturgeon. The bait should be placed directly on the bottom, as they feed on bottom-dwelling creatures and fish. The most favourable times are before the sturgeon migrate to spawn, and after reproduction, before they set off to return to the sea.

Characteristics

Spindle-shaped, with naked skin and an asymmetrical tail fin, the sturgeon makes a shark-like impression. The head is protracted to form a long beak (rostrum) and bends slightly downwards at the end. The lower lip of the downward facing, toothless mouth is split and has four round, smooth barbels (fleshy filaments). The back is bluey-grey, the flanks silvery-grey and the belly whitish.

The best bait

Fish are the best bait to catch sturgeon, particularly if you have set your sights on one of the larger specimens. Bottom-dwelling species are preferable as baitfish, as sturgeon prey on them under natural conditions, too.

In waters where sturgeon do not thrive so well, worms, snails, mussels and insect larvae can be used as alternative bait, as sturgeon devour bottom-dwelling creatures of more or less every kind.

Bleak

Other names: Willow-blade

DE: Laube, Ukelei,

FR: Ablette,

ES: Alburno, NL: Alver,

SE: Löja, PL: Ukleja

Distribution

In Europe, bleak are to be found from the Volga to western European waters. They do not occur in the Mediterranean region, northern Scandinavia, Ireland or Scotland, and they are rare in Wales and the West Country.

Bread flake or dough is a good choice of bait for this small fish.

Bleak inhabit just about all still and slow-running waters, and they even find their way into the brackish waters of the Baltic Sea. They do not like habitats where there is vegetation, and in fact, they actively avoid such areas, preferring to remain in open waters near the surface. They also like to remain near the banks. Under optimal environmental conditions, bleak will quite often form large shoals. As they remain largely untroubled by water pollution or by depleted oxygen supplies, bleak are also frequently to be found under less than favourable conditions.

The best bait

It is not easy to choose the right bait as bleak live on plankton for the most part. Their food intake is supplemented to a small extent by plants and insects that drop onto the surface of the water.

Hemp seed, cheese, bread, dough and small dry flies produce good results as well as small dungworms, maggots and grasshoppers.

Bleak

Characteristics

The bleak is an elongated fish with flattened sides and a long anal fin. The back varies in colouring from greeny-blue to greeny-grey, and the flanks are silvery. The mouth is upward facing, reflecting their pattern of feeding from below. Except for having a longer tail fin, bleak resemble—and may be mistaken for—dace.

with light tackle close to the surface and pre-baiting with light, loose groundbait are the best means to success. Bleak are a particularly good fish for beginners. They are not at all timid and take the bait greedily—a good opportunity to train bite recognition and striking.

Light, loose feed that spreads easily attracts bleak to the fishing location.

Their spawning period lasts around three months, beginning in May. The male has a spawning rash the entire time, even into the month of June. Bleak mostly lay their eggs in shallow areas near the bank where the bottom is sandy or gravelly. If this is not possible, the bleak displays its accomodating nature by simply laying its eggs on plants and roots. Each female lays up to 12,000 eggs, between 1.5 and 1.9 mm in size.

The average length of a fully-grown bleak is between 10 and 15 cm, and even those specimen that do reach the maximum length of 25 cm seldom weigh more than 100 g. For this reason, they are only really of interest to anglers as baitfish.

The best time to catch bleak is between March and August, especially in mid-summer. Float fishing

The best way to catch bleak is with light tackle close to the surface.

Brown Bullhead

DE: Katzenwels, FR: Poisson chat,
ES: Pez gato, NL: Amerikaanse
dwergmeerval, SE: Brun dvärgmal,
PL: Sumik karłowaty

Distribution

Little is known about the distribution and population of the brown bullhead. Originally indigenous to the eastern USA, they were introduced to Europe at the end of the nineteenth century. Now they are found in western, central and eastern Europe. The family of the brown bullhead includes around 40 varieties. In Europe, you also find the black bullhead (Ameiurus melas)—mainly in Italy—and the channel bullhead (Ictalurus punctatus) in southern England.

Characteristics

The brown bullhead is a scaleless, moderately elongated fish with an adipose fin. The fins—all grey-brown to black—are rounded. The back is black to olive-brown in colour, the belly whitish, while the flanks display darkish mottlings. The brown bullhead has four pairs of long barbels (fleshy filaments) and a broad, terminal mouth.

You can find worms, snails and freshwater shrimps at your fishing spot to use as bait.

Brown bullhead are gregarious, nocturnal bottom-dwellers and are very sensitive to pollution. They tend to live in lakes and large ponds with clear water and dense vegetation. Reports of brown bullhead sightings in polluted waters are probably due to the brown bullhead being confused with another member of this large family, such as the extremely robust channel bullhead (*Ictalurus punctatus*).

Bullhead are no longer introduced anywhere because they eat fish spawn and are classified as a pest.

Their spawning period lasts from April to July. The parent fish build a simple nesting hollow from plant material where the eggs are laid in sticky balls. The spawn and the fry, which hatch after four to six days, are watched over by the male. The fry like to stay in shallow, warm waters, forming cluster-like shoals. Brown bullhead reach an average size of 20 to 30 cm; the maximum reported length is 48 cm.

Anglers wishing to hook this fish can use the evening and night hours and outwit the brown bullhead with a light bottom hook. Bait should be presented on or close to the bottom.

The best bait

Brown bullhead naturally feed on mosquito larvae, snails, fish spawn and small fish. Baitfish and scraps of fish therefore make excellent bait. Alternatively, worms of every kind can also be used.

Eel

Fine eels can be caught using dead baitfish offered on the bottom.

Even today, eels are considered something of a mystery: there are still many unanswered questions regarding their spawning behaviour and development. On average, eels measure 40 to 60 cm, at a weight of 500 g. They can reach lengths of up to 130 cm and there have been reports of specimens weighing over 5 kg. Females grow much larger than males, and most eels over 45 cm long are females.

Eels leave inland waters in late autumn to visit their spawning grounds in the Sargasso Sea in the north Atlantic. The female eel lay some 500,000 eggs per kilo of body weight at depths of 150 to 500 m, at a water temperature of around 19 °C (66 °F). This number of eggs at first appears astronomically high. But when you consider that eel roe are only 0.12 mm in

DE: Aal, FR: Anguille,
ES: Anguila, NL: Paling,
SE: Ål, PL: Węgorz

Distribution

In Europe, you can find eels in almost all waters right up to the Urals, where they live along the coasts and in estuaries and the rivers that flow into the sea there as well as their tributaries. Eels have now either colonised those regions where they did not originally occur, or have been introduced, as in southeastern Europe, for example.

Eel

The eel does not only hunt on the bottom.

Characteristics

Eels have an extended body, elongated like that of a snake. Their very slimy skin seems naked, as their scales are not only very small, but also deeply embedded. The back is very darkly coloured and the belly, which has no fins at all, is white to yellow, depending on their stage of development. The tail fin and anal fin are continuous. The head is either very broad or pointed, depending on their diet: plant eaters have a smaller head, while predatory eels have a wide head.

The best bait

Eels can be caught very successfully using small fish, fish scraps and various kinds of worms. Crab and shrimp are also effective. Detailed knowledge of the waters and feeding habits of the local eel population are crucial for successful catches.

Eels basically live on insect larvae, worms and small crabs. Their diet seldom varies as long as the food supply remains adequate. If it does not, eels will increasingly turn to fish for food, in which case the head of the eel changes shape from elongated to broad.

diameter, it becomes credible. Eels only spawn once in their lifetime and die after the reproductive act is over.

Once the young eels have hatched, they migrate to inland waters over a period of about three years. By the time they approach the European continental shelf, they are around 7 cm long (at this stage they are called "elvers"). Upon their arrival, they change their appearance within 24 hours from leaf-like to the typical eel shape. It is not yet known what triggers this spontaneous transformation. What does seem certain, however, is that it occurs where the water is less than 1000 m deep. The young eels now resemble the adults in appearance,

but still lack their pigmentation: they are transparent, which is why at this point they are called "glass eel". In addition, at around 6 cm, they are now somewhat shorter than before their transformation. But they are outstanding swimmers, sometimes covering 8 km in a single day while heading for the brackish coastal waters.

Once there, however, they do not immediately enter fresh waters, as their metabolism still has to adapt. The various factors governing which rivers the glass eel choose have not yet been completely established. It is, however, certain that they do not eat during this time and that the pigmentation process only begins as they swim up river.

Being nocturnal, during the day eels mostly remains motionless in

Eel

their hideouts. They like to stay under the roots of dense underwater vegetation and hollowed-out banks. Only at nightfall do they set out to hunt for prey. It is important for anglers to know the typical hideouts and hunting grounds in each respective habitat. Between mid-April and the end of October is the best time of year to fish for eels. Besides at night, eel will often bite on warm, humid summer evenings and during light rain or thunderstorms in the daytime. Legering and float fishing have proved effective; the bait should be presented on or close to the bottom. To catch large eels, it is best to use fish as bait and make sure that the tackle is not too light. Use a steel leader, as other predatory fishes may well go for the hook too.

Heavy eels weighing several pounds need to be pulled in hard, otherwise it is all too easy for them to wriggle their way into snags.

Eels feel most at home on or in soft mud on the bottom.

Asp

DE: Rapfen, FR: Aspe,
ES: Aspio, NL: Roofblei,
SE: Asp, PL: Bole

Distribution

In Europe, the asp is most frequently encountered in the east, with the Urals probably being the furthermost limit. They can be found as far north as southern Sweden and the south of Finland. Some regions are not so favoured owing to the decreasing number of suitable spawning grounds; to some extent, this has been remedied by mixed stocking.

Asp feel most comfortable where there are currents and basically only live in large rivers or lakes, which have rivers passing through them. However, asp have been successfully stocked into lakes that do not have a connecting river, and feel quite at home there provided there is a good current flow. Young asp like to form shoals and to remain near the water surface. As they grow older, they increasingly become loners. This distinguishes asp from other European cyprinids (members of the minnow and carp family), as they are the only ones to live solely as a predator.

The male asp displays a prominent rash throughout the spawning period, from April to June. Asp go upstream to spawn, and look for sandy or gravelly locations where there is a rapid current. Here, at water temperatures of between 5 and 10 °C (40–50 °F) each female lays more

Asp

Even a small asp will snap at relatively large prey.

Characteristics

Asp have an elongated body which is slightly flattened at the sides. The back ranges in colour from dark olive to bluish, the sides are silver and the belly white. The deeply incised mouth is slightly upward facing, with a protruding lower jaw. Asps have grey-reddish fins and small eyes.

The bubble float allows you to cast further and present bait close to the surface.

Asp usually remain near the surface of the water or at medium depths. Only the particularly large specimens are sometimes to be found deeper down. In general, asp always like to stay in the current, behind obstacles. It follows that good places for catching them are directly behind breakwater heads or the piers of bridges.

The best bait

Twisters and small weighted spinners are the best bait for catching asps. Big flies (streamers), wobblers and pirks can be used as alternatives. As the adult fish like to eat small fish, baitfish and fish scraps should also be considered as options.

than 100,000 eggs, each of which is 1.5 mm in diameter.

Asp grow very rapidly and by the time they are only one year old can be as long as 20 cm. Their maximum length is normally 80 cm, at a weight of 5.9 to 7.9 kg. However, individual specimens weighing around 12 kg and 1.2 m in length have also been reported. On average, asp grow to lengths of 40 to 70 cm at an average weight of 2 to 3.6 kg.

The best time to catch asp is between July and August: in hot summer months, they can be outwitted by surface fishing with a bubble float, or spin fishing.

Double-tail twisters are particularly attractive bait for asp.

Barbel

DE: Barbe,
FR: Barbeau,
ES: Barbo de río,
NL: Barbeel,
SE: Barb,
PL: Brzana

Distribution

Barbel are to be found from the Black Sea to the Atlantic Ocean; their eastern limits are Lithuania and White Russia. They are absent from parts of the Mediterranean, Italy, the Iberian Peninsula and Scandinavia. In Great Britain, barbel are primarily confined to rivers in the south, east and Midlands. In France they occur in the north-east, the east and the south-west. Because weirs and dams now often prevent their spawning journeys barbel numbers are declining in several regions.

The habitat of choice for barbel is largish rivers which have sandy or gravelly beds. They inhabit regions where the current is moderate—this is why they are mostly to be found in the middle reaches. Barbel are gregarious and prefer to live in small shoals. During the day time barbel tend to remain in hideouts in the current, setting off at twilight to look for food. They often cover distances of several miles when travelling through their home waters.

Barbel reproduce between May and July. They gather in large shoals before heading upstream to their spawning grounds. During this period, the male has a spawning rash on the head and neck, consisting of white vesicles arranged in rows. Barbel perform their mating on gravel banks where the water is shallow and fast-running. The female scatters up to 10,000 eggs measuring 2 mm in diameter into the gaps in the gravel. The hard roe of the female barbel is poisonous, causing nausea and diarrhoea if eaten. This would seem to be some form of natural protection for the eggs.

When the fry hatch after around two weeks they spend an additional ten days in hollows on the river bed, as they need this time to learn to swim. An average

Barbel

The best bait

Barbel can be angled with a wide variety of bait. As well as lobworm and redworm, bundles of dungworm are very effective. But cheese has proven to be the best bait, particularly varieties such as Limburger, Stilton, or others with a strong smell. Maggots, luncheon meat, raw sausage meat, snails and meat loaf are also successful. Where the current is weak, it is also worth trying dough or bread flake.

Natural foods for barbel are insect larvae (preferably mayflies), small shrimps, fish spawn, algae and, to a lesser extent, small fish. You can, of course, also use any of these as bait if they are obtainable.

Barbel have a tough mouth, so hooks have to be particularly pointed and sharp.

barbel tips the scales at 1 to 3 kg and is 30 to 50 cm long. Really large specimens can be up to 90 cm long and weigh around 10 kg.

To catch these fish, legering or float fishing with light or medium tackle is the best approach, during the evening hours or at night. You have the best chance of catching barbel between April and October, provided you know their favourite haunts. It is always worth trying stretches of river with a fast current that are located near calmer parts. You should also try places where obstacles such as rocks or abundant water plants obstruct the current. Barbel can be caught behind weirs and turbines and in deep river pools, as well. It is important to present the bait right on the bottom, as they usually remain very deep down.

Characteristics

Barbel are round-bodied fish. The back is brown or greenish, with lighter flanks and a white belly. Its large fins are grey-green to reddish. The longest ray of the dorsal fin is bony and serrated. It has a large downturned mouth with thick lips and four barbels on its upper lip.

Cheese cut into cubes is easy to put on the hook.

It is good to have alternative baits to hand, as cheese is not always the barbel's first choice.

17

Silver Bream

Other names: White bream

DE: Güster, Blicke,

FR: Brème bordelière,

ES: Brema blanca,

NL: Kolblei,

SE: Björkna,

PL: Krąp

Distribution

In eastern Europe, silver bream are to be found all the way to the Urals. They occur almost everywhere in France and in all the Benelux countries. Although they are found throughout Germany, in the British Isles they only occur in East Anglia. Silver bream are completely absent from the Mediterranean Sea and Italy, and only live in the southernmost regions of Scandinavia.

Silver bream are quite often confused with the common bream. This is not only because of their very similar appearance, but also because the two fish share other characteristics. Just like the common bream, silver bream prefer to inhabit slow-running or standing waters with muddy bottoms. They also like to form shoals, so it is not surprising that silver bream join with common bream to form larger groups.

Silver breams' preferred environments are in the vicinity of river banks with heavy vegetation and in blind river arms in the lower reaches. They even make their way into the brackish waters at river mouths. Lake fish seldom venture far away from the zones of marginal plants near the shores. As silver bream often occur in very large numbers, over-population is

frequent. If food becomes generally scarce as a result, the fish develop stunted forms.

From May to June, silver bream gather near the banks to reproduce. The male displays a slight, very fine spawning rash. They are not particularly fussy about what they spawn on, although they prefer

These bottom-dwelling fish can be caught with light tackle and the right instinct.

Silver Bream

Characteristics

Silver bream are deep-bodied fish, strongly flattened at the sides, with a short dorsal fin and a long anal fin. They have a relatively small head with protruding eyes. The distance from the front edge of the eye to the end of the snout is the same or less than the diameter of the eye. The mouth cleft is terminal or slightly downward facing and cannot be protracted to form a proboscis. They have large fins. The paired fins are mostly reddish near the base. The back is dark, and its flanks and belly are light with a silvery sheen.

bream reach a length of 15 to 20 cm; the largest specimens can be up to 35 cm long.

May to September is the best time to catch silver bream. It is most effective to use sweetened groundbait and legering or float fishing with light tackle. Shallow stretches of water with abundant vegetation, preferably near the bank, are the best fishing spots. The bait should be presented on the bottom, as that is where the silver bream forages for food.

Wheat boiled until soft can be used both as bait and groundbait.

dense vegetation. The female lays up to 100,000 eggs, 1.6 mm in diameter, which adhere to the bottom; laying is done in a shoal, with much splashing about as an accompaniment.

Silver bream grow relatively slowly and are often only 8 to 10 cm long at the age of three years. However, they are often already sexually mature despite their small size. On average, silver

The best bait

Maggots are the best bait for silver bream. Casters (the chrysalis stage of maggots), small worms, dough, sweet-corn and cereals are also good.

Of course, you can also try everything which silver bream eat under natural conditions. They prefer plant debris and small water creatures such as fresh-water shrimp, but will also eat blood-worm (also called tubifex), insect larvae and other bottom-dwelling worms.

Casters are a delicacy for all silver bream.

Crucian Carp

DE: Karausche,
FR: Carassin,
ES: Carpín,
NL: Kroeskarper,
SE: Ruda,
PL: Kara

Distribution

Originally, crucian carp were mainly to be found in the Caspian Sea and the Black Sea up into the temperate zones of northern Asia. Nowadays, they are very widespread, occurring in an area stretching from the Lena river system in Siberia to western Europe. However, they are absent from north and west Scandinavia and the British Isles. In the Mediterranean crucian carp only appear in the southern half of the Iberian Peninsula and the north of Italy.

Shallow waters with abundant vegetation are ideal living conditions for this fish.

The crucian carp is amazingly resistant and insensitive to cloudy waters. They make themselves at home in any sort of standing water, which they prefer to be full of reeds and vegetation. They make use of soft, muddy bottoms: in extremely dry periods they will bury themselves in the mud and are then often the only species able to survive. In such cases, however, a lack of natural enemies may lead to over-population and stunted growth. Crucian carp avoid strong currents and therefore the only flowing waters they inhabit are the sluggish waters of very small ponds and ditches.

Crucian carp require a water temperature of no less than 15 °C (60 °F) in order to reproduce, which usually takes place between May and June. Then they gather in shallow areas near the shore in large groups, where they spawn together. Each female lays up to 300,000 eggs from 1 to 1.5 mm in diameter.

An average crucian carp grows to be 15 to 25 cm long at maturity and weighs between 250 and 500 g. In spite of occasional rumours of enormous crucian carp which are 75 cm in length, the maximum recorded size is just 40 cm long and 1 kg in weight.

The best time to catch crucian carp is between July and October. The early hours of the morning and early evening are most favourable. The best methods are legering or float fishing using light tackle, with the bait presented directly above the bottom.

The best bait

In their natural surroundings crucian carp prefer to eat small bottom-dwelling animals, but also feed on parts of plants and dead plant material. Maggots and sweetcorn have proven to be the best bait, though worms, pieces of dough and potatoes and boilies can also be used, as the fish will bite well at these, too.

Characteristics

Crucian carp are deep-bodied fish that look pressed together at the sides. The back is dark grey-green, the flanks brownish and the belly a yellowy bronze. The slanted, upturned mouth, convex dorsal fin and a black spot at the root of its tail are also characteristic. Crucian carp have no barbels, which is how it can be distinguished from the common carp.

Beaked Carp

Beaked carp are found exclusively in flowing waters. They live in the middle reaches of rivers, often together with barbel. Beaked carp are also unusually sensitive to pollution levels in their habitats. Young beaked carp prefer to stay in backwaters that are protected from the current and, like the adults, tend to form large shoals.

Characteristics

The most distinctive feature of these fish is undoubtedly their protruding beak with a downturned mouth and lips that are horny at the edges. It is also called a "pig's snout". The beaked carp's almost cylindrical body is only slightly flattened at the sides, making a cross-section look like a rounded oval. The back varies in colour from grey-green to brownish; the flanks are lighter with a silvery sheen.

Shoal formation also plays a major role during the spawning period from March to May. The fish gather into shoals and head off upstream to their favourite spawning grounds. It is characteristic of beaked carp that both sexes display a spawning rash during this phase. Strong currents and a bouldery bottom are important for reproduction. Here, the female lays up to 100,000 eggs of 2 mm in diameter, which adhere to the ground. The male only fertilizes the eggs after they have been laid. It takes ten to 16 days for the fry to hatch. Like their frequent companions the barbel, it takes another ten days before they can swim. The largest beaked carp, which can be 50 cm long and weigh 1.5 kg, are rarely seen. The majority weigh between 250 g and 1 kg and are 40 to 50 cm long.

The best time for catching beaked carp is between June and October. However, they do bite very well in winter as well, provided the weather is not too cold. A light leger rod with a running sinker or a light float-fishing rod is the right tackle to use. The bait has to lie on the bottom to outwit the fish.

The best bait

Beaked carp live mainly off algae growing on stones, and only eat small amounts of bottom-dwelling fauna, so choosing the right bait is not easy. Maggots (the best bait of all), small worms and insects, cheese, bread and dough fished on the bottom can all be effective.

DE: Nase,
FR: Hotu,
ES: Nasudo
NL: Sneep,
SE: Noskarp,
PL: winka

Distribution

Beaked carp are found in a broad region extending from the Urals to southwestern France. They occur everywhere from the Netherlands to Switzerland, with the exception of the Elbe basin in Germany. But they are absent from the Mediterranean region, the British Isles and Scandinavia.

At least five subspecies have been identified in Europe, most of them in isolated waters in the Balkans.

Grass Carp

Grass carp have a very hard mouth, making it difficult for a hook to penetrate—so hooks need to be especially sharp and pointed.

DE: Graskarpfen, Amur
FR: Amour blanc, carpe amour, ES: Carpa de la hierba, NL: Graskarper, SE: Gräskarp,
PL: Amur biały

Distribution

The grass carp's natural habitat is east Asia. They were introduced to Europe in the 1960s. But nowadays because they are no longer released as often, their numbers vary from region to region.

The silver carp (Hypophthalmichthys molitrix) and the bighead carp (Hypophthalmichthys nobilis) belong to the same group of fish, commonly known as grass fish. However, in European waters these varieties are of no importance to anglers.

Despite their name, grass carp do not belong to the carp family but, like the other varieties of so-called "grass fish", are a part of the group of true whitefish of the genus *Leuciscus*. Grass carp are found in lakes, dams, ponds, rivers and shipping canals, inhabiting the slow-running zones and preferring shallow areas with abundant underwater flora.

It has been suggested that this type of fish does not reproduce in Europe at all, as they require a water temperature of at least 20 °C (68 °F) for spawning. The optimum temperature for grass carp is 22 to 29 °C (72 to 84 °F),

Grass carp are happiest in dense vegetation like this.

conditions that are seldom reached in European waters. However, since grass carp do indeed occur in all kinds of different countries and waters, yet have only rarely been released into the wild, this would seem to indicate that natural reproduction does take place at least sporadically.

Grass Carp

Boilies enriched with spinach are good grass fish bait.

Grass carp journey upstream to spawn, where they look for gravelly stretches with fast-running water. After the eggs have been laid they swell up so they can float. While the spawn is being carried downstream by the current, the fry hatch within one or two days, feeding at first on plankton. When they reach a length of about 3 cm they begin eating plants, becoming purely vegetarian when they have grown to just over three times this size.

Grass carp reach a maximum length of 1.2 m and, in Europe, attain weights of around 35 kg. In their native habitat in eastern Asia, where they grow very fast in the warmer waters and may already have reached half of their maximum length after their third summer, they can be up to 50 kg in weight.

The best bait

Thanks to their knife-shaped, serrated pharyngeal teeth and their digestive system, grass carp can break down and digest even the hard parts of plants. As this diet is not very nourishing, grass carp have to eat up to 120 per cent of their body weight every day, but they remain strictly vegetarian.

This makes grass carp difficult to catch, as the choice of bait is somewhat limited. Boilies are the most successful bait; they should contain a high proportion of sweetcorn and be enriched with additives such as spinach or water plants (made into fine flour). Sweetcorn is second on the list of successful bait, but potatoes, dough and pieces of reed can also be used as alternatives.

Characteristics

Grass carp are cylindrical, elongated fish with a broad, downward-facing mouth without barbels. The back is a brownish-green colour, while the flanks are a lighter green or shiny grey and the belly white. The grass carp's large scales have dark edging at the back, creating a visible net-like pattern. All of its fins are short and coloured dark grey. The dorsal fin is rounded.

You can go angling for grass carp anytime between May and September, but the months of July and August are to be preferred. These fish can be caught at all times of the day, although at night they tend not to bite so well. Areas with dense water foliage, mainly in relatively shallow zones, are good fishing spots. You should use legering or float fishing with medium-weight tackle, and employ a pop-up bait, presented close to the bottom.

The silver carp also belongs to the grass fish family, but is of little interest to anglers.

Carp

Other names: Common carp, king carp, gold carp, leather carp, line carp, mirror carp, scaled carp

DE: Karpfen, FR: Carpe, ES: Carpa, NL: Karper, SE: Karp, PL: Karp

Distribution

The area from which wild carp spread throughout Europe seems to have varied according to climatic conditions and therefore can no longer be reconstructed exactly. It seems certain that carp were introduced to the cooler parts of Europe at the time of the Roman Empire. Nowadays, wild carp are to be found all over Europe up to the Urals, except for north-western and north-eastern Scandinavia; this is also true of the ornamental forms.

The barbels and the openings to the side of the eyes can be seen clearly – both of them help the carp find food.

Carp are the basic form of the *Cyprinidae* family. In addition to the common carp, there are at least four ornamental varieties of carp in European waters. Common carp are to be found both in lakes and rivers. In general, they are able to adapt to the conditions in their home waters, however extreme those may be. They can even tolerate very low levels of oxygen, although carp naturally are more comfortable under optimal conditions. They occur both in standing waters and slow-flowing waters. Carp like warm temperatures and seek out sandy or muddy bottoms. A predilection for abundant vegetation is also characteristic: carp prefer to live amongst underwater plants, under carpets of water lilies and so forth.

Warmth and aquatic plants are also important to carp in their reproductive cycle. As a general rule the spawning period is between May and June, but in the end the exact timing depends

Carp

Characteristics

The wild carp is an elongated fish, while the ornamental forms (mirror carp, leather carp, line carp and scaled carp) are more deep-bodied. All varieties have blue-grey to black backs, brownish to greeny-yellow sides and a golden yellow belly. The protrusible mouth with four barbels (fleshy filaments) and strong, spiny rays on the dorsal fin and anal fin are also shared characteristics. Scaled carp and wild carp are completely covered with scales. Mirror carp have large scales distributed unevenly. Leather carp have no scales, while line carp have a single row of scales along the lateral line.

Carp like to stay at the surface or at a medium depth.

on weather conditions, and sometimes the carp may not spawn until as late as July. In particularly warm summers, the fish might even spawn a second time. As soon as the water has reached a temperature of 18 °C (64°F), carp head for the warmest parts of the water, near the banks.

It is imperative that there be enough vegetation in carp spawning grounds, as the eggs are laid on parts of plants. River-dwelling cyprinids need flooded areas to

Carp

A scaled carp swims just above the bottom.

Zebra mussels grow in small clumps and are a favourite food.

reproduce: during the spawning period they leave the flooded river and tend to mate over grassy areas in water that is at most 40 cm deep. In addition, there are varieties of carp living in brackish water in the Caspian Sea and Black Sea that journey to the flood plains of the lower river reaches in order to spawn.

Each female carp lays 200,000 eggs, 1.6 to 2 mm in diameter, per 500 g of body weight. Laying the eggs often takes place over a period of several days and at different sites. The female is not satisfied with one male: up to fifteen may be employed. Theoretically at least, it would be possible to watch carp reproducing, as they lose all timidity and reserve, letting almost nothing disturb them. The fry hatch after three to five days and start off eating plankton. As soon as they reach a length of around 2 cm they begin digging up the bottom in their search for food.

Cultivated forms of carp reach an average length of 40 to 60 cm and weigh between 2 and 5 kg. The maximum length can be as much as 120 cm, with a maximum weight of 30 kg. Carp may grow to be very old: 50-year-old specimens have been known.

Generally speaking, the best time for catching carp is between March and December. In flowing waters the season runs from March to mid-April, then again

The fish is not in the net yet—as an angler you should count on a final struggle.

from July until December. The starting point depends on when the weather allows the fish to begin spawning and when the spawning period has finished.

In standing waters, the best time to catch carp usually starts between two and four weeks later, and ends in November. The reason for this delay is quite simple. The lakes in which the carp likes to live are often very deep and thus it takes longer for the water to warm up in springtime. As carp not only need warm water to reproduce but generally have a preference for it anyway, it takes longer for them to become really active in standing waters. In addition, they use less energy in still waters than they do in rivers, where they have to fight against the current.

It is often said that carp become active at twilight and prefer to stay deep down during the day. This is only true to a certain extent, as these fish are very capricious. The carp's behaviour is heavily dependent on the conditions in their home environment. There are countless factors that influence how carp behave, so if you want to continue to achieve good catches over an extended period of time, you will have to oberve them closely.

The best bait

The carp's staple diet consists of bottom-dwelling creatures such as insect larvae, worms, snails, small mussels and crustacea. Young fish eat animal plankton, and adults also eat water plants, if only in small quantities.

There are many ways of getting carp to bite but over the past few years boilies have proven to be the most successful bait. The important thing when catching carp is to know what sort of food naturally occurs where you are fishing so that you have enough alternatives should your supply of the best bait run out. As well as the other typical carp baits—such as worms, potatoes, dough, sweetcorn, bread, chickpeas, tiger nuts, pellets and even cat and dog food—it pays to keep your eyes open and use everything that nature provides.

Carp can be caught at any time of the day or night. The above-mentioned places where carp like to stay are always good spots to catch them. Pre-baiting has proven to be efficaceous. Legering and float fishing with bait presented close to the bottom are effective, as is surface fishing with floating bait.

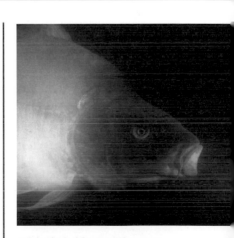

With their big mouths, carp have few problems finding something they can eat.

Pike

The pike has many sharp teeth that can only be tamed by a steel leader.

The fact that pike are distributed over an extremely large area should make it immediately obvious that these are highly adaptable fish. Their preferred habitats include clear waters with gravelly bottoms; the water can be either still or slow-running. Pikes' favoured places are near the banks with plenty of contours and abundant vegetation. Lakes that are slightly cloudy in summer are also suitable.

Pike have the ability to adapt their colouring to their surroundings, making them barely visible despite their substantial size. These fish are very flexible in other ways, too, and adjust well to the conditions around them. Pike living near coasts, for example, may often be found in brackish waters. Pike also inhabit bodies of water in mountainous regions at altitudes of up to 1,500 m.

Pike

DE: Hecht, FR: Brochet, Lanceron, ES: Lucio, NL: Snoek, SE: Gädda, PL: Szczupak

Distribution

Pike are the most widely distributed freshwater fish of all, being found in large parts of northern North America and Asia as well as in Europe. Here it is absent from the Mediterranean region, northern Scotland, Iceland and western Norway. On the Iberian Peninsula, it only occurs from the lower reaches of the Tagus River (in Portugal) to around Talavera de la Reina (Spain); otherwise, it is ubiquitous.

The pike is a diurnal fish and a voracious predator. They normally wait motionless in their hideouts for potential prey to come along, generally in shallow spots near the bank where they can hide well in vegetation. Here, they stay near the surface and wait until the right prey comes within their reach. Then they shoot out suddenly, as quick as a flash, and snap. If they miss their prey, they usually do not go in pursuit of it, but hide once more to wait for the next opportunity to present itself.

Fish living in a big lake are sometimes also found in open waters, where they tend to remain near large shoals of fish; this gives them a good chance of catching another fish if the first one gets away. Pike have little stamina and do not swim fast. This is not such a big problem, however, as they are not fussy about what they eat. They prefer fish from the carp family, but will take just about anything that comes their way. They do not restrict their diet to fish: frogs and water birds may also become prey. If the population of pike increases to a level where it becomes difficult to find food, pike will even turn cannibal. This is a simple and effective way of solving over-population problems.

Pike have a mouth full of small backwards-pointing teeth. This ensures that their prey cannot escape

Pike prefer to wait for their prey hidden amongst aquatic vegetation.

Characteristics

Pike have an elongated, cylindrical body and "duck-bill" jaws bearing numerous sharp teeth—these can be truly dangerous for the unwary angler. The lateral line extends to the base of the tail, but is interrupted several times. The pike's back is coloured dark green to blackish and its sides have grey-green-yellow stripes, often with golden patches. The dorsal fin is situated far back.

Pike

Good catches are possible with large wobblers.

The best bait

Young pike eat nothing but plankton until they are 5 cm long. Then they turn their attention to fish of every sort, and basically hunt anything that crosses their path, such as frogs, water birds and small mammals. In waters densely populated by other pike, they develop cannibalistic tendencies.

For predatory fishes like pike, it is best to use fish as bait. If you have none handy, try using all sorts of spoons, spinners, wobblers, plugs or rubber fish.

once seized by a pike—in itself a very useful adaptation. However, in some cases these teeth may cause problems for the pike. If a pike has caught an animal that is actually too large for it, the fish is unable to spit it out again. The worst case scenario would be that the pike might even suffocate; but more commonly you will encounter a pike with a fish hanging partly out of its mouth, while the rest has already been mostly digested.

The spawning period for pike begins in February and lasts until May. During this phase, pike tend to head for flooded areas or shallow spots near the banks with dense vegetation. Female pike can lay over 300,000 eggs and they mate with two or three males. The eggs are between 2.5 and 3 mm in diameter and are very sticky, allowing them to adhere to water plants. Pike grow very rapidly and can attain a length of over 30 cm in their first year if enough food is available. On average, they are 40 to 80 cm long. Really big ones can be 1.5 m in length and weigh over 20 kg.

The best months for catching pike are from September to January and then May. Places where small whitefish occur in shoals—offering themselves to the pike on a plate, as it were—are the most favourable. You should also look for good pike hideouts, such as patches of vegetation, hollowed-out banks, submerged wood and so on. It is best to fish for pike during the day and in the early hours of morning and evening. Legering, float fishing and spinning are all effective techniques, but a steel leader must be used with any kind of rod because of the pike's strong teeth.

The optimal fishing depth depends on the position of the respective shelter or hideout.

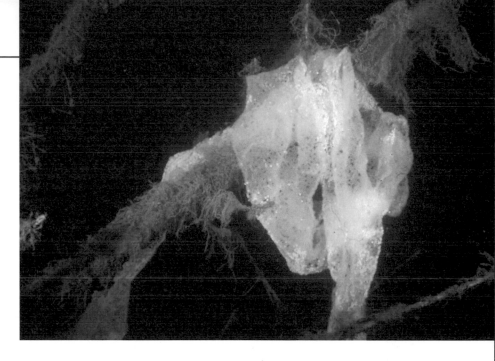

Pike lays their eggs in big clumps.

Specimens of this size are wonderful surprises.

Ruffe

Other names: Pope

DE: Kaulbarsch, FR: Gré-
mille, goujon-perche,
ES: Acerina, NL: Pos,
SE: Gärs, PL: Jazgarz

Distribution

In Europe, ruffe are found from north-eastern France to the Urals. They do not occur south of the Pyrenees and the Alps, in the Crimea or in the Balkans. There are no ruffe in Ireland, Scotland, Norway nor in north-western Sweden. In the UK they are limited to the Midlands, south England and a small area of Wales.

Ruffe thrive in habitats that offer them calm water and sandy bottoms. Therefore you are most likely to encounter them in slow-running rivers. They are also found in large numbers in lakes and large ponds, as well as in the brackish waters at river mouths. Ruffe do not even shy away from the areas of the Baltic which have a lower salt concentration. They like to live in large shoals near the bottom, but also occur in flowing waters in the lower reaches of the trout zone.

The ruffe's spawning period extends from March through May. They are not particularly fussy about where they spawn, but do require a water temperature between 10 and 15 °C (50 to 59 °F). Eggs of about 1 mm in diameter are laid near the bank at a maximum depth of 2 m. Each female ruffe lays approximately 400 eggs per gramme of body weight, either singly or in strings. The eggs are attached to plants, stones or the bottom. Then they are fertilized by several males which have followed the female. When the fry hatch after five to 15 days, their eyes do not yet have any pigmentation, only gaining their colouration two days later.

Ruffe

A good way to catch ruffe is to use small fish traps.

Typical bottom-living creatures—such as insect larvae, freshwater shrimps and worms—form the majority of the ruffe's natural diet. They also enjoy fish spawn. Therefore the best baits are redworm and maggots. Ruffe will also bite well on red wrigglers and various insect larvae.

Where freshwater shrimp are numerous, ruffe are sure to be close by.

On average, a fish of this species reaches a length of 10 to 20 cm and a weight of 50 to 100 g. Ruffe grow to a maximum length of 25 cm and a maximum weight of 250 g. Ruffe are often an unintentional catch, as they usually take the bait very greedily and swallow the hook deeply. If you do specifically want to catch them, you can do so all year round, although the best times are shortly before and after spawning. Use light legering or float-fishing tackle with light hooks and live bait, and you should be successful. To attract ruffe to the fishing spot, muddy the water, using a stick, for example. Try using small maggots, such as pinkies, as groundbait.

Characteristics

Ruffe have a dorsal fin with sharp spiny rays. The back is brown and irregularly covered by blue patches on a greenish background. The belly and flanks of this slightly hunch-backed fish are a whitish yellow, while the tail fin has dark spots. Ruffe have a large, rather pointed head with proportionally big eyes and a turned-up snout. The scales are rough. The ventral and anal fins have single spiny rays at the front.

Pinkies are good groundbait for this little predator.

Use a catapult to cast the groundbait.

Danube Salmon

DE: Huchen, Donaulachs
FR: Huchon,
saumon du danube,
ES: Salmón del Danubio,
NL: Donauzalm,
SE: Donaulax,
PL: Glowacica dunajska

Distribution

In Europe, Danube salmon occur almost solely in the Danube and some of its tributaries. They have now been released into a few other rivers—in central and eastern Europe, for example, where you may find isolated populations.

Danube salmon thrive where the water is cool and well oxygenated. For this reason, they live mostly in rivers with gravelly and stony bottoms. Danube salmon are very territorial, defending their domain against all comers. They prefer to stay in deep waters where there is a strong current.

Their spawning period runs from March to April. During this time, the male Danube salmon develops a kype, that is a hook-like lower jaw. The male also develops thicker skin. All these changes are necessary because there is violent competition at the spawning grounds. The fish head upstream or into small tributary streams, but travel relatively short distances. Strong currents and shallow, well-oxygenated water are

Danube Salmon

Characteristics

Danube salmon have an elongated, almost cylindrical body, and a long head, flattened towards the top, with a mouth extending behind its eyes. The jaws have strong teeth; the first gill arches have 16 to 18 gill rakers. They have a relatively large adipose fin, while the other fins are all quite small. The back is of a brownish-violet colour, while the flanks are lighter with a coppery or violet sheen. Back and sides are patterned with numerous black spots. The belly is a shimmering silvery-white, and the tail fin is distinctly notched.

important for spawning. Once the Danube salmon arrive, they build spawning hollows on suitable gravel banks. The female lays up to 25,000 eggs that are 5 mm in diameter. After the eggs have been laid, the spawn is covered up with gravel. Because of their late spawning period, the fry develop much faster than those of other salmonids, as the water is already warm.

On average, Danube salmon grow to a length of 80 to 100 cm and weigh 5 to 10 kg. Large specimens of 160 cm in length, weighing 52 kg, have been reported, but these only occur in the Danube River.

To catch Danube salmon, it is best to try from October to February and directly after the spawning period. Strong spinning rods or leger rods with strong lines and a steel leader are recommended. Hollows in the banks, deep river pools and places behind big stones are good spots to catch Danube salmon. The bait should be presented close to the ground.

It is not easy to get Danube salmon to bite. When they do, however, they put up a hard fight and make considerable demands on the angler. As Danube salmon make excellent eating, though, it is certainly well worth the effort.

Large slender wobblers tempt the Danube salmon to bite.

The fisherman's chances of success improve at twilight.

Rubber bait is a cheap alternative, especially in waters where there are likely to be snags.

The best bait

Young Danube salmon eat all kinds of invertebrates and any available small fish. From their second year of life onward they feed mostly on fish, but will also take frogs, water birds and small mammals.

The best bait of all for Danube salmon is the so-called "Hucho plait", a special spinning bait made of strands of leather or rubber braided together. If you do not have one handy, baitfish, large spinners, twisters and rubber fish are all effective. Dark wobblers can always be used. Spoons, which are often used for other fish, are not so attractive to Danube salmon. If you do use them though, they should be silver or golden in colour.

Pumpkinseed

DE: Sonnenbarsch,
Sonnenfisch
FR: Perche-soleil,
ES: Perca sol,
NL: Zonnebaars,
SE: Solabborre,
PL: Bass stoneczny

Distribution

Originally indigenous to eastern North America, the pumpkinseed was introduced to Europe at the end of the nineteenth century. They were generally known as aquarium fish and their release into the wild may have happened for various reasons or even may have been unintentional. There are now numerous populations, varying widely in size according to location, in eastern, central and western Europe.

The male is only this brightly coloured during the spawning period.

The waters where pumpkinseed live must be clear and clean. They prefer relatively shallow water and abundant bottom vegetation, which means that in temperate zones they are most often found in small, shallow lakes and ponds. Pumpkinseed also occur in large lakes or rivers, provided these are slow-moving and have sufficient small aquatic creatures. They live in blind arms of rivers and lakes that are warm in summer, for instance. Pumpkinseed spend most of the year at depths of between 1 and 2 m; it is only in winter that they withdraw to deeper areas. Generally they like to remain near the bottom. Pumpkinseed can pose a serious danger to the local fish population as they eat young fish and fish spawn, among other things. In locations where pumpkinseed have few natural enemies and there is over-population, they tend to develop stunted forms.

Pumpkinseed spawn between May and July. During this time, the male, in particular, displays beautiful colouring. The normally pale hues on its head turn into shimmering blue or green stripes, and the gill-cover spot also seems to gain in brilliance. The male's back is gold-green with reddish brown mottling, and the belly is reddish brown to orange. The shimmering yellowy green flanks have reddish brown and blue patches, and even the dorsal fin has spots.

Pumpkinseed only spawn when the sun is shining. When the water temperature climbs above 16 °C (62 °F), the male looks for suitable spots on the margins to dig a fairly simple nesting hollow. Each nest is defended by a territorial male, even though the hollows are all very close to one another. Pumpkinseed usually spawn near an abundance of bottom-dwelling flora at depths of 15 to 50 cm. Every female lays up to 5,000 eggs, which have a diameter of 1 mm, in a spawning hollow. After this, both parents guard the hollow

You can attract pumpkinseed with juicy maggots.

The best bait

In their natural surroundings, pumpkinseed feed on small invertebrates including worms, small crustacea, insect larvae and food that drops onto the water surface, but they also eat fry and spawn. Small fish and maggots have proven to be the best bait for pumpkinseed, however. Scraps of fish, worms, very small spinners and even fish spawn provide enough alternatives.

Characteristics

Pumpkinseed are deep-bodied fish, strongly compressed laterally: older specimens appear to be almost disc-shaped. The short head has a small, terminal, slightly upturned mouth that does not extend back under the eye. The gill covers have a rounded extension at the back which looks like an ear and which sports a black spot outlined with red and white edges. Pumpkinseed are relatively colourful, but both sexes are paler outside the spawning period than during it. They have medium-sized ctenoid scales, a continuous lateral line and an undivided dorsal fin with spiny rays at the front. The ventral fins and anal fin also have spines, but only singly.

and will even attack considerably larger fish. Pumpkinseed grow to a maximum length of 30 cm and seldom weigh more than 1 kg.

To catch pumpkinseed you need light tackle: a small fixed-spool reel, thin monofilament lines and small single hooks. A leger rod or float rod should be used in shallow waters with a lot of vegetation or shelter such as sunken branches. Groundbaiting with maggots or fish spawn is effective. The hook bait should be presented on, or close to, the bottom.

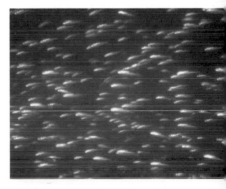

Places where there are shoals of small fish provide the pumpkinseed with plenty to eat.

Chub

Snails are a great delicacy for chub.

DE: Döbel, Aitel,
FR: Chevaine,
ES: Bagra,
NL: Kopvoorn,
SE: Färna,
PL: Kle

Distribution

Chub are widespread almost all over Europe, with their eastern limit being the Urals. In Scandinavia, they are only to be found in the south of Sweden and Finland and throughout Denmark. They are absent from Ireland, Scotland and southern Italy.

Chub live mainly in rivers, as they prefer flowing waters, though they will also reside in lakes and reservoirs with natural inlets. Being very resistant to environmental pollution, chub often dominate the fish population in polluted waters. Young chub live in shoals, sometimes together with dace. Their lifestyle may be described as pack behaviour: like wolves, young chub have a leader of the pack—this is always the largest fish in the shoal. However, as they grow older, chub become predatory loners. Adult chub choose one location to live in and defend these territories, which are mostly sheltered places near the banks.

The chubs reproductive period begins in April and lasts until June, and is initiated with short spawning journeys. During this phase, the males display a fine-grained spawning rash. In small shoals, the fish look for places in the current above gravelly bottoms.

Profile of the head of a chub.

Cherries and other fruit are particularly good bait for catching chub.

Characteristics

Chub are elongated, with an almost cylindrical body. The back is a dark brown-green. They have a thick-set head with a turned-up snout and deep-cut mouth. The flanks are silvery with a yellow sheen, and the belly is the same colour without being glossy. Its rough scales have black edges. The edges of young chubs' fins are convex.

There, the females lay their sticky eggs: 46,000 eggs per kilo of body weight. Each egg measures 1.5 mm in diameter. Spawning takes place over the course of 10 to 20 days in two or three sessions. The fry hatch approximately eight days later, which means that the parents are still busy reproducing while their first progeny are already out and about.

On average, adult chub are 30 to 40 cm long and weigh up to 1 kg. The maximum length is 70 cm and they can weigh anything up to 5 kg.

Chub can be caught all year long, but success depends heavily on the time of year and the method used. In summer, chub generally position themselves near the water surface, whereas in winter, chub remain in deep water—not directly in the current, but a few yards further downstream, where the water is somewhat calmer. You also have a good chance of catching chub behind bridge piers, under overhanging trees and behind large stones. But bear in mind when choosing bait in summer that chub have a semi-vegetarian diet at this time of year.

The best bait

Young chub eat both plants and invertebrates of all sorts, but also fish spawn. Older chub like to eat fish, crustacea and amphibians, but they too become semi-vegetarians in the summer.

There are numerous possible baits for catching chub. It is impossible to say which is best, as these fish take very different baits depending on the time of year or the method used to catch them. The usual baits such as worms, small fish, bread or dough, sweetcorn, large insects, spoons, wobblers, wet and dry flies are all possible.

But it is certainly worth your while to try unusual treats such as small frogs, cheese, luncheon meat, liver, pasta, peas, cock-chafers, slugs and fruit. Of the fruits, cherries have proven to be a particular delicacy for chub.

Orfe

Other names:
Ide, golden orfe

DE: Aland, FR: Orfe, ide
mélanote, ES: Cacho,
NL: Winde, SE: Id, PL: Ja

Distribution

Orfe can be found all over eastern and central Europe with the exception of to the west and south of the Danube and Rhine systems, in Ireland, and central and northern Norway. In Great Britain, the orfe is only encountered in the south and the Midlands (as well as in ornamental pools). In central Europe it even occurs in the Baltic, but its numbers are declining in the south of the continent.

Orfe are often confused with chub, despite having a narrower mouth (see picture on p. 38).

Orfe prefer to live in large rivers, where they like to stay out in open water. But they are also at home in large bodies of standing water, provided these have strongly contoured banks, and even in the brackish waters of the Baltic. Orfe have a tendency to form shoals at every stage of their life, and look for food in open waters. Orfe are very active fish that undertake long migrations in the course of a year. Although it has some-times been said that large orfe live as predators, there is to date no firm proof to substantiate this claim; it may be a case of chub being mistaken for an orfe.

Orfe migrate upstream in order to reproduce between March and May. Lake fish make do with shallow spots near the shores. As long as the bottom is gravelly, this causes no problems. They remain gregarious during this phase of their life cycle; it is only after spawning that they adopt a solitary

Orfe

Heavy orfe fight hard against light tackle.

lifestyle. Each female lays up to 100,000 eggs of 1.5 to 2.3 mm diameter onto the gravel. Orfe may deposit their eggs on water plants or tree roots, but this is the exception rather than the rule.

Characteristics

Young orfe are often confused with chub or dace, but if you observe them closely you will see that they have a narrower mouth and smaller scales, and their anal fin has an indented edge. Orfe are fairly deep-bodied fish with nine rows of scales above the lateral line. The back is brown to blackish blue, the flanks light and silvery, and the belly white. The dorsal and caudal fins are grey, and all other fins are slightly reddish in colour. The corners of the mouth are slightly downturned.

A spawning rash is typical of the male orfe.

Orfe reach an average length of 30 to 50 cm, tipping the scales anywhere between 250 g and 2 kg. The heaviest known specimens have weighed 6 kg and measured 80 cm in length.

The best time to set off to catch orfe is between June and October. Using light legering or float fishing tackle, you can usually outwit them near the surface in summer. In spring and winter, they remain deeper underwater, so you should present the bait close to the bottom instead. Good fishing spots are places in the current: for example, behind stakes and bridge piers, near breakwater heads or above sand banks.

The best bait

Natural foods for young orfe are plankton and food that has dropped onto the water surface. Older fish also like to feed on worms and the larvae of insects such as mosquitoes, but do not turn their noses up at small crustacea and snails .

The best baits for orfe are maggots and worms, but there many possible alternatives. In addition to insects, compost worms, small boilies, dough, bread and caddis fly larvae, you should also try artificial flies, cooked wheat and even peas.

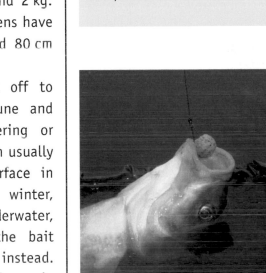

This orfe could not resist a boilie.

Dace

Other names: Graining
DE: Hasel, Märzfisch,
FR: Vandoise, assée,
ES: Cachuelo, NL: Serpe-
ling, SE: Stäm, PL: Jelec

Distribution

Dace are widespread in Europe, missing only south of the Pyrenees and Alps, in northern and western Scandinavia. Dace have a wide distribution in England, but are uncommon in Scotland, west Wales and the south-western peninsula. They have been introduced to Ireland. Dace are found all over Germany, in greater numbers towards the south. Dace from the Rhone, Adour and Garonne regions are sometimes mentioned as a species in their own right: Leuciscus igelensis or burdigalensis.

Be alert and ready to respond to careful bites when float fishing.

D ace prefer flowing waters with fast currents, but are also to be found in calmer zones. They particularly like clear water with a gravelly or sandy bottom. In lakes, they tend to remain near the inlets. But since dace are among the very adaptable kinds of fish, they also inhabit less favourable waters, provided the water is not too cold: the temperature needs to reach at least 18 °C (64.5 °F) in summer. Dace will often form shoals, often together with chub. They general-ly wait near the surface of the water for insects and other food to land there.

The spawning period begins in March and lasts into May. The male does not take on any special colouring at that time, simply dis-playing the rash typical in fish of the carp family. In order to reproduce, dace require a water temperature of 9 °C (48 °F) or more. They then migrate upstream, often travelling for several miles. They spawn in groups above gravelly bottoms in the current. Each female lays up to 12,000 eggs that are about 2 mm in

Dace

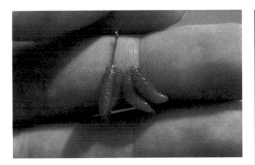

Put the maggots onto the hook carefully so that they wriggle temptingly for the fish.

Characteristics

Dace are not particularly striking in their colouring. The blackish blue back, white belly and silvery flanks are typical of all whitefish. The slender to slightly stocky body with a maximum of seven or eight rows of scales above the lateral line is also characteristic of dace; the scales are, however, large. The ventral and anal fins are light grey to yellowish, whilst the dorsal and tail fins are grey. The outer edge of the anal fin is slightly concave when it is spread. Dace have an ever so slightly upturned mouth.

diameter. They are fertilized immediately by the male. Once the eggs have been evenly distributed by the current, they remain attached to the bottom.

The dace is one of the nimblest and fastest members of the carp family. On average, they measure 15 to 25 cm in length, and their average weight is around 250 g. Really large specimens are rather rare, but they have been known to reach 30 to 40 cm long and over 500 g in weight.

Most anglers would rather not catch dace as they have a lot of bones, which makes them anything but popular as an eating fish. If you do wish to catch them, however, it is best to try between June and October. But it is also worth trying in winter. A light fly rod or float rod, with the bait presented near the surface, should do the trick. Remember that dace are very timid. Always move quietly and cautiously near the water so as not to frighten them away.

The best bait

Dace eat a wide variety of food and adapt to what is available. Although they prefer small invertebrates and insects that land on the surface of the water, they will also eat plants (such as blanket weed), insect larvae and worms.

Fishing for dace shows just how important it is to take a close look at the home waters of a particular species of fish, because the success of the bait used depends on the food that naturally occurs there. Dungworms, small red wrigglers and maggots are usually good, and you cannot really go wrong with bread and dough either. But you should definitely try everything that creeps or flies near the water (such as grasshoppers). When in doubt, you can also make do with small dry flies (those used in fly-fishing).

Small worms and colourful dough are good dace bait.

Burbot

Other names: Eel pout

DE: Quappe, Trüsche,

FR: Lote, barbotte,

ES: Lota,

NL: Kwabaal,

SE: Lake,

PL: Miętus

Distribution

Burbot occur just about everywhere in Europe. There are a few small exceptions in certain localities: for example, in Italy they are only to be found in the Po Valley. In Great Britain they are confined to the eastern rivers and are quite scarce.

Burbot are predatory creatures. They are the only member of the cod family to live and reproduce solely in freshwater. They prefer to live in clear rivers with firm, gravelly or sandy beds. However, they are also to be found in well-oxygenated lakes that remain fairly cool in summer. During the day, this nocturnal fish with a reduced swim bladder hides away on the bottom, so it needs waters that provide plenty of places to shelter in. After nightfall, the burbot starts its hunt for prey. Particularly in salmonid waters, it is considered a pest, as it eats spawn and is mainly active during the colder months of the year.

Depending on where their home waters are situated, burbot reproduce from December to February or November to March. Burbot form shoals to begin their long

Burbot

Characteristics

The burbot is an elongated fish. Its back and sides often have very pronounced mottling. Its basic colouring is greeny-brown, while the belly is yellowy-white. The burbot has a long, strong barbel on its chin and two short ones on its upper jaw. Its first dorsal fin is very small, while the second dorsal fin and the anal fin extend to the rounded tail fin. Burbot have a broad, flattened head with a slightly upturned mouth.

spawning migrations upstream, which often cover distances of more than 100 km. Generally, burbot prefer to spawn above sandy bottoms in deep waters; but they will also accept stony bottoms as a spawning substrate. The female lays up to one million yellowish eggs 0.8 to 1.5 mm in diameter. Each contains a drop of oil (with a diameter of around 0.4 mm), which allows spawn in lakes to develop while floating in open waters. In flowing waters, however, the eggs adhere to the bottom, where the fry hatch after six to ten weeks.

Burbot reach an average length of 20 to 60 cm, but the largest known specimens have been up to 1 m in length and have weighed as much as 5 kg.

The best time to angle for burbot is the period before and directly after spawning, although they can be caught successfully throughout the winter. Stormy nights with falling rain or snow following severe periods of frost are particularly favourable. Legering with a running sinker and presenting your bait on the bottom during the night when the fish are waiting for prey should prove effective.

Small baitfish are best of all for these small predators.

The best bait

The young fish eat bottom-dwelling invertebrates. When the fish have reached a length of 20 to 30 cm, they start feeding on small fish for the most part. But they are not averse to spawn, something that has given burbot a bad reputation.

To catch burbot, it is best to use baitfish, but lobworm and redworm, liver and chicken gut have all proven to be very effective bait as well.

Burbot are not choosy when it comes to shelters.

Burbot particularly go for thick bundles of worms.

Large-mouthed Black Bass

Other names:
Largemouth bass

DE: Schwarzbarsch,
FR: Black-bass à grande
bouche, ES: Black-bass,
perca americana,
NL: Zwarte baars, forel-
baars, SE: Öringsabborre,
PL: Bass wielkogębowy

Distribution

*A native of North America,
large-mouthed black bass
were introduced to Europe
in the last century. These
days, they are very wide-
spread, particularly in the
south. There are two species
of black bass that were
introduced, but the small-
mouthed bass (*Micropterus
dolomieui*) is rarely seen in
European waters, as it prefers very cold water. Records
are imprecise, but there are
said to be large populations
to the south of the Alps, in
the Alps themselves, and in
the Pyrenees.*

In contrast to their close relative, the small-mouthed bass,
large-mouthed black bass prefer
much warmer waters. They can be
found in large, calm lakes or rivers
that contain clear or only slightly
clouded water. When they are
young, large-mouthed black bass
live among the water plants
in shallow areas near the bank.
Older fish are territorial and
live deeper down, mostly between
stones, plants or sunken wood,
where they lie in wait for their
prey. In general, the large-mouthed

bass's behaviour can be viewed
as a combination of that of the
perch and that of the pike, as it
lies in wait for its prey at times,
but also goes on the hunt in
small groups.

Large-mouthed black bass reproduce between March and July.
Males dig a shallow ditch that
they defend as their territory.
These spawning hollows are
situated in sandy ground about
1 m under the water surface.
After the female has laid several
batches of eggs, the males guard

Large-mouthed Black Bass

The large-mouthed black bass likes living in waters like these.

Large-mouthed black bass also hunt for prey near the surface.

both the spawn and the fry, as soon as they hatch approximately one week later. Each female lays around 10,000 eggs per kilo of body weight, and often mates with several males.

The large-mouthed black bass reaches an average length of between 40 and 60 cm, though exceptionally large specimens can be more than 90 cm in length and weigh up to 10 kg.

Between July and October is a particularly good time for landing large-mouthed black bass in your net. But be aware that you can only be really successful if you know the waters very well. The large-mouthed black bass stays in a number of different hideouts, and also at different depths. So you need to consider anywhere that could be used as a hiding place down to a depth of 12 m.

If a hiding place is large enough, several fish may even be secreted there at once. Therefore it is a good idea to return to such locations to fish over a period of time, especially if there is a good stock of large-mouthed black bass in the waters. Another possibility is to fish near the surface using bait that generates a great deal of noise. But even then, you will be more successful if there is a bass sheltering place lower down.

For both techniques—spin fishing and legering—you will need medium tackle, although if you use rubber bait a fairly stiff rod is advantageous. The line should generally be very strong, as largemouth bass put up a very hard fight.

Characteristics

Large-mouthed black bass are powerful, slightly deep-bodied fish with a large head that takes up more than a quarter of their body length. They have a very deep-cut, upturned mouth, and the gill covers extend at the back to form a spur. The ctenoid scales are very small, the dorsal fin is deeply notched (almost divided in two), and only the front, much lower part has spiny rays. The back is dark and mottled, its sides yellowy green and marked with a broad, dark, lengthwise stripe that sometimes breaks up into spots. The belly has a slightly reddish silvery sheen.

The best bait

This fish also eats a wide range of food that includes all sorts of aquatic creatures as long as they are the right size. Adult large-mouthed black bass mostly live on small fish, while the young fish feed on insects and their larvae, crustacea and even plankton.

Baitfish, fish scraps and rubber fish have proven to be particularly effective forms of bait. Spinners, small spoons, wobblers and twisters also give good results.

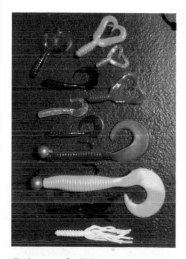

Twisters of all kinds tempt the large-mouthed black bass.

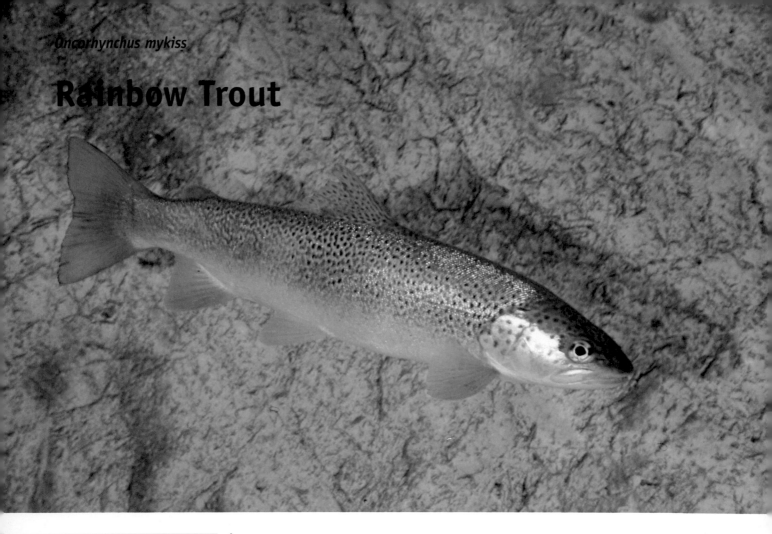

Oncorhynchus mykiss

Rainbow Trout

Other names:

Steelhead trout

DE: Regenbogenforelle,
FR: Truite arc-en-ciel,
ES: Trucha arco iris,
NL: Regenboogforel,
SE: Regnbågslax,
PL: Pstrąg tęczowy

Distribution

Although the rainbow trout was not native to Europe originally, they are now to be found everywhere in the temperate climate zones. This is largely because it was used to stock many fisheries, but there are now populations that reproduce naturally in certain regions, for example in Germany.

Rainbow trout like flowing waters, so their natural preference is to live in rivers and streams. However, because their occurrence in Europe is mainly the result of stocking, they can also be found in lakes, reservoirs and ponds. Rainbow trout are not territorial and move about within large areas. They are not particularly timid, and will also hunt in open waters, although they mainly feed near the bottom at depths of up to 10 m. Rainbow trout prefer foaming water under waterfalls, deep channels and the countercurrents at river bends.

Basically, the rainbow trout is much less sensitive than the brown trout, as it can tolerate warmer water and does not seem to

have any great problems with poorly oxygenated water. If the waters otherwise provide good conditions, this fish can cope with temperatures of around 22 °C (72 °F) in summer; and even if the water is temporarily warmer than this, rainbows suffer little ill effect.

This is only true, however, if the fish are stocked early on in life. Rainbow trout one year of age and more or that are fully grown have great difficulty coping with these conditions. Unfortunately, this kind of stocking, which is done to make the waters in question more attractive for anglers, is all too common. The fish, accustomed

Coloured dough is good bait for rainbow trout when trolling.

Rainbow Trout

to artificial food, are almost starved before being introduced into the new waters, as they would otherwise barely react to the baits offered. If they are not caught first, these fish are likely to suffer a bitter fate: already weakened by hunger and temperature shock, they are scarcely capable of adapting to the new conditions. They easily fall prey to illnesses (such as fungal infections) and finally die.

When rainbow trout are stocked in a reasonable manner, however, because of their comparative hardiness they are normally released into waters where their relation, the brown trout, has more or less disappeared. This is not only the case in waters where the water

Characteristics

Rainbow trout are elongated fish, slightly compressed at the sides. They have a blunt snout and an adipose fin. On the first gill arches, only the middle gill rakers are raised as small rods. The back is a blue-grey, with reddish violet shimmering flanks and a silvery belly. The entire fish, except for its underside, is covered with a large number of small black spots. The tail shaft is flattened and fairly high.

As the original, wild rainbow trout from North America evolved through breeding, several subspecies developed. Various characteristics, such as the shape of the body, the number of vertebrae and the colouring can therefore vary a great deal.

Concentration is needed, as the rainbow trout often strikes with unexpected force.

Rainbow Trout

Salmon roe is good bait, but hard to put on the hook.

Rubber frogs make an unusual but often very effective alternative bait.

The rainbow trout puts up a very good fight.

quality has diminished, but also where straightening of the river has deprived this fish of the necessary places to shelter.

It is not easy to establish exactly when rainbow trout reproduce, as this depends on the breed. What is more, most of the information we have is based on trout reproduction in their place of origin, North America. Rainbow trout are able to reproduce in the wild in Europe, but attempts to establish a population are seldom successful, and the same can be said of its natural reproduction. The spawning period lies between November and May. At first, females looks for a suitable site with sand or gravel. Here, they start digging a ditch, while the males court them—provided

they are not occupied with driving away other prospective suitors. As soon as the spawning hollow is ready, the male follows the female into it and they deposit the eggs and milt side by side. After this, a second male fertilizes the eggs. The female now begins to dig another spawning hollow next to the first one, which is covered up with the sand or gravel dug out from the new hole. In each spawning session, 700 to 4,000 eggs are laid which are 3.5 to 6 mm in diameter. By the time the female has laid all its eggs (around 2,000 per kilo of body weight), the reproduction ritual has been repeated over a period of several days.

In its place of origin, the rainbow trout reaches a length of

Rainbow Trout

The best bait

Young rainbow trout eat plankton and invertebrates. Older specimens feed on fish, amphibians and their spawn, as well as insects and bottom-dwelling creatures (such as crustacea) of all kinds.

This means you have a wide choice of bait. The most effective baits are worms, dough and wet or dry flies. You can also use small spinners, small wobblers (in rainbow colours), small spoons and imitation frogs made of rubber. Maggots, sweetcorn, grasshoppers and coloured salmon roe are also good. Metal lures should be silver or golden if possible; if using a dough, the types that swell up are more successful.

130 cm and can weigh up to 15 kg; in Europe, the fish are on average 30 to 50 cm long and weigh 5 kg. They grow very fast, which means they sometimes represent a serious threat to the local fish population in the waters they inhabit. They eat not only other fish and their spawn, but are even prepared to eat their own species.

The best time for catching rainbow trout is between July and September. The best equipment to use is a medium-weight fly rod or spinning rod. Good fishing spots are hollowed-out banks, overhanging trees and river pools. The best depth at which to present the bait will vary anywhere from near the surface all the way down to depths of 10 m.

Where it is permitted to fish with spinners, these lures tend to be very effective.

Perch

Other names: Redfin perch, crutchet, frasling, hurling

DE: Flussbarsch, FR: Perche, ES: Perca, NL: Baars, SE: Abborre, PL: Oko

Distribution

In Europe, perca fluviatilis is the member of the perch family you are most likely to encounter and the most widely distributed. It occurs from western Europe to Siberia, except in the extreme north of Scotland and parts of Scandinavia. Perch are not found in mountain streams, nor are they found in Portugal and the Mediterranean region. In Spain they only occur in the north-east.

Wobblers are good for catching large perch.

Experts trick the fish into biting using sparkly jigs.

Perch are not particularly demanding with regard to the waters they inhabit. This explains their wide distribution and why they are so frequently encountered. They can be found in standing and moving waters, and the only places which they avoid are small, shallow lakes and streams that are very muddy. Perch inhabit rivers up to their upper reaches, and even in the Baltic's brackish water perch are not only numerous, but sometimes grow extremely large. They live in rivers and lakes at high altitudes, as well, and can be found at heights of up to 1,000 m above sea level.

Their behaviour patterns and diet are as varied as the waters they inhabit. However, they show a marked preference for the warmer reaches of waters that have sufficient depth, a slow current and a solid bottom. Nevertheless, perch can be found in all sorts of different places. Whether out in the open at various depths, or in near the banks—this fish can and does turn up anywhere and anytime.

Young perch tend to form shoals, as do the smaller adults of the species. Perch only grow really large when they live in deep waters, which, however contain comparatively little food. Otherwise they remain small and stunted, so it is not surprising that you can find sexually mature perch that are less than 10 cm long.

Perch shoals have a tendency to remain near the bank or in shallower zones, such as those above underwater mounds, so much so that they are known as "perch hills". If the waters they inhabit allow them to reach their maximum size, however, the fish turn into loners that stay mainly deep down. They live increasingly as predators, even eating their own species. Normally perch lie in wait behind tree roots, near break-

Perch

water heads or in similar hiding places, but they are genuine hunters and will go in pursuit of their prey deliberately. Perch are not tied to one location and move around a great deal. But they return again and again to their favourite places, so their behaviour is very much intertwined with their environment.

Things become really interesting in large bodies of water that are full of underwater structures.

Characteristics

Perch have a laterally compressed body that often becomes hump-backed as the animals age. Its back is dark green, while its sides vary from a brassy yellow to greenish colour and are marked with between five and nine broad, black, vertical stripes. The belly is silvery white, sometimes with a reddish shimmer. The perch has a blue-black patch on the first dorsal fin, which has strong spines. The ventral fin, anal fin and rear dorsal fin have single spiny rays at the front. The fins are mostly reddish, but can also be yellowish in some cases. Other characteristics of the perch are its rough ctenoid scales, the medium-sized terminal mouth, and the pronounced spur on its gill covers.

Perch

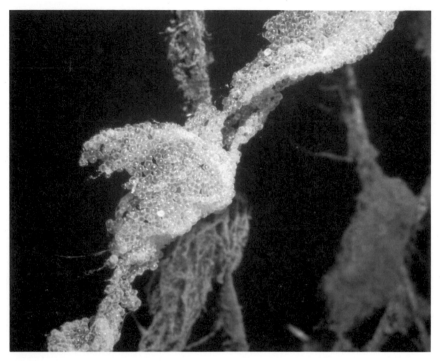

Perch spawn in ribbons.

Small perch in particular are very gregarious creatures.

In such a setting you will not only find large and small perch and both forms of behaviour, but also diverse combinations, such as groups of large perch that hunt together.

Perch reproduce between March and June. They need a water temperature of 7 to 8 °C (45 to 46.5 °F). The fish look for areas above aquatic plants, stones or other objects such as sunken wood. Each female lays about 200,000 eggs, which are imbedded in long ribbons of a jelly-like material. These ribbons, which are up to 2 cm wide, are deposited all over the spawning substrate. The spawn

Perch

is fertilized immediately after it is discharged. Several males may take part in this procedure. The fry hatch some two or three weeks later.

Perch grow very slowly by comparison to other fishes. Their average length is 15 to 35 cm; however, any perch longer than 30 cm is generally 15 years of age or more. The longest recorded specimens have measured 50 cm and weighed around 3 kg.

Perch can be tempted to bite all year round, but the very best time to angle for them is at the height of summer and in autumn. A light to medium-weight leger, float or spinning rod should be used. The strength of the equipment called for depends mainly on your choice of bait, which should not be too small, as perch like biting on relatively large objects. The bait should be presented at different depths and at a variety of spots, depending on the waters and the size of the perch that occur there. If spin fishing is your method of choice, the perch often bite at a jerking bait. It is advisable to use a fine steel leader, as pike usually inhabit the same type of waters that perch do.

The best bait

While young perch live on plankton and small bottom-dwelling fauna, adult perch prefer small fish, fresh-water shrimp, insects and worms.

Perch bite best at all types of spinners, jiggers and twisters. They also seldom turn their noses up at small baitfish. Alternatively, you can use casting spoons, wobblers, raw meat, maggots, pieces of fish and lobworm or redworm.

Head shot of a several-pound perch.

Banks that are practically inaccessible are always good for a surprise catch.

Roach

DE: Rotauge, Plötze,
FR: Gardon, ES: Rutilo,
NL: Blankvoorn, SE: Mört,
PL: Pło

Distribution

Roach are to be found almost all over Europe, with their eastern limit being Siberia. They do not occur in regions south of the Alps and Pyrenees, in north-western Scandinavia, or in the upper reaches of streams or in mountain lakes. They are also absent from the Mediterranean, where the southern European roach (Rutilus rubilio) is found instead. The red roach (Rutilus arcasii) and several other subspecies or anadromous forms also occur in the north-west of the Iberian Peninsula.

Roach are very insensitive to pollution. They prefer standing or slow-running waters, but because of their adaptability they can also live elsewhere. Roach like to form shoals and to stay in zones near the bank where there is plenty of vegetation, in underwater plant beds, or in reed banks. They prefer shallow to medium depths. At greater depths, only the largest specimens are encountered, mostly on the bottom, where they even occasionally live as predators.

The size to which roach grow depends on the food supply available to them. If there are enough small animals such as molluscs and snails, the fish become deep-bodied; otherwise they remain rather slender, even tending to be stunted if there is a lack of fauna for food.

Roach spawn between April and May; however, this activity can extend into June depending on weather conditions. In larger, flowing waters roach undertake spawning migrations. During this period the male displays more intensive colouring and a spawning rash on its head and body. Roach spawn noisily in large shoals in shallow areas with abundant vegetation. Each female lays over 100,000 eggs, 1 to 1.5 mm in diameter, which adhere to plants, roots or similar objects.

When the fry hatch after five to ten days, they cannot swim for

Roach

Characteristics

Roach may have a high-backed shape or a more slender form, depending on the food available to them. The basic colouring of these fish is silvery with a green-ish or bluish dark back. The white belly is slightly reddish during the spawning period. The dorsal, pectoral and tail fins are grey-red. The ventral and anal fins, which are barely keeled or not at all, are orange to red in colour. Between these fins, the fish has rounded scales. The base of the ventral fin is vertically under that of the dorsal fin. The iris of the eyes varies from orange to red.

The roach is not very particular about where it lives.

another three to eight days until after they have consumed their yolk sacs. On average, roach will grow to be 15 to 30 cm long and weigh up to 500 g, with the largest specimens weighing 1.5 to 2 kg. Roach over 40 cm in length are an exception.

Roach bite particularly well in July and August and from September to November, but they can certainly be caught all year round. Legering and float fishing with light tackle—i. e., a thin line and a small hook—are the best methods. They can also be caught throughout the day. The most favourable spots are shallow coves, landing stages, reed patches and underwater plant beds. Attract the fish first using loose balls of tangy or spicy cloud groundbait.

A roach seldom lacks for company.

The best bait

Roach eat a wide variety of food, including insects and their larvae, plant remains, plankton, small molluscs, snails and invertebrates of all kinds. What they eat depends on what is available in the waters they inhabit. Large roach will occasionally also hunt and eat small fish.

Maggots, casters (maggot chrysalises) and hemp seed have proven to be the best bait when fishing for roach. If they do not work on occasion, there is a wide range of alternatives. As well as the usual delicacies such as worms, larvae, dough, pieces of potato and white bread flakes, it is worth trying algae, wheat, or a combination of sweetcorn with casters and maggots.

Legering with a feeder is also a good way to get roach to bite.

Salmon

DE: Lachs,
FR: Saumon,
ES: Salmón,
NL: Zalm, hengst,
SE: Lax,
PL: Łoso

Distribution

Salmon live in the coastal regions of the northern Atlantic and in the North Sea and Baltic up to northern Scandinavia and northwestern Russia. This is where salmon have their spawning grounds. Sometimes, though rarely, they are found in the lower reaches of these rivers even outside the spawning period. In Lake Ladoga and some other lakes in the north-west of Russia and Scandinavia, there are also purely freshwater populations. However, significant populations of salmon only remain in Ireland, Scotland and Scandinavia.

Salmon are an anadromous fish, meaning that they normally live in saltwater but travel to fresh water in order to reproduce. Within their normal habitat, they prefer to remain near the coast, though they also undertake long journeys. Salmon are mostly found at depths extending down to 10 m.

From October (in northern Europe) or November (in central Europe), salmon visit the river systems where they grew up, and spawn at sites with a moderate current and clean gravel bottom in cold water. Here, too, they remain true to the places they know, mostly returning to their parents' spawning beds. During this phase the male salmon

takes on beautiful colouring and—something that is important in view of the violent fights that take place between rivals—grows the typical kype, or hooked jaw, which forms during the ascent to the spawning waters. The spawning hollows are dug by the female at a depth of about 1 m, and can be up to 2 m in diameter. Spawning rituals include a prolonged courtship display, spawning in pairs and the covering of the hollows after the act has been concluded. The female can repeat this process over several days—sometimes with different males—until she has laid all her eggs (around 20,000). Most salmon die after spawning. The few sur-

Salmon

Characteristics

When fully grown, salmon have a grey-brownish back, a silver-white belly and light grey flanks with a few prominent black spots. Young salmon, on the other hand, have dark spots or vertical stripes. The colour of the flanks turns silvery at the beginning of their migration to the sea. Salmon have an elongated body with a very thin tail shaft. The ventral fins and dorsal fins are situated approximately in the middle of the body. The fish have powerful teeth and an adipose fin. Their deep-cut mouth extends behind their eye.

The Atlantic salmon is an imposing fish.

vivors travel back to the sea and will reproduce again after one or two years.

On average, salmon grow to a length of between 50 and 100 cm and attain a weight of 1.5 to 10 kg. There have been reports of salmon as big as 150 cm long and weighing over 40 kg.

In fresh water, the main period for catching salmon is between May and October. The exact time depends on when they begin their migration, as the fish have a sort of reflex during the first weeks that makes it particularly easy to lure them onto a hook. However, in contrast to other anadromous fish species, they do not stop eating completely even during the rest of their ascent. When fishing for salmon, you need medium to heavy tackle, as these fish have proven to be very good fighters. A spinning rod or fly rod is best for catching them.

The best bait

The best bait for salmon is without question baitfish, as the adults' natural diet consists solely of other fish. Large salmon flies and spoons have also proven to be successful lures in some situations.

Salmon start eating other fish as soon as they have attained a length of about 10 cm. Before this, the young fish feed on insect larvae, freshwater shrimp and other invertebrates.

Large, light-coloured streamers are good for catching salmon.

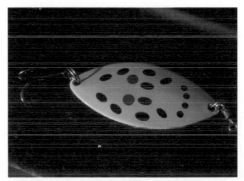

You can also use large spoons to angle for salmon.

Brown Trout

DE: Bachforelle,
FR: Truite de rivière,
ES: Trucha da río,
NL: Beekforel,
SE: Bäcköring,
PL: Pstrąg potokowy

Distribution

Brown trout are the most widely distributed members of the extensive trout family, and stem from various subspecies of the sea trout. Brown trout occur throughout Europe, including Iceland; the only place from which they are absent is the south to the south-west of the Iberian Peninsula. Populations are relatively good everywhere, most likely as a result of continual stocking.

Brown trout are quite demanding with regard to the waters they inhabit. They require highly oxygenated, fast-flowing water that is very cold. They are happiest in waters that remain cool in summer and where the water temperature does not climb above 18 °C (64.5 °F) for any extended period of time. As they grow older, brown trout become increasingly territorial: once they have taken up residence in a particular domain, they barely leave it, defending it against all intruders. They prefer to stay among roots and similar objects that can serve as hideouts. They are also very fast swimmers with a great deal of stamina, and consequently move around a lot. Sometimes they will even jump out of the water to catch flying insects.

The timing of the brown trout's reproduction depends on where they are living. Those fish living

in higher regions (such as mountain streams) are the first to spawn, as early as October. The lower the altitude of their home waters, the later they reproduce—sometimes delaying until March. The fish migrate upstream, where the female digs spawning ditches by beating its tail against the gravel bottom in waters where there is a strong current. After the eggs have been laid—each female lays around 1,500 eggs per kilo of body weight—the ditches are covered over again.

As a rule, brown trout grow to a length of 20 to 40 cm and weigh

Mealworm is a particular delicacy for brown trout.

Brown Trout

Characteristics

Brown trout are elongated, torpedo-shaped fish. Their basic colouring is quite variable. All types are characterised by black or often red spots, mostly with white or blue edges, on the flanks. When young, brown trout also have dark vertical stripes.

The adipose fin most commonly has a reddish edge, and the tail fin is only very slightly indented. The brown trout has small scales, a large head and numerous teeth. Its mouth extends to behind its eye.

125 to 500 g. Individual brown trout seldom reach the maximum length of 50 cm or the heaviest weight of 5 kg. In fact, in mountain streams at high altitudes they are seldom longer than 15 cm when full-grown.

Brown trout bite particularly well between May and September, but it is worth trying all year round. Very good results are to be had with light spinning or fly tackle under overhanging branches, under bridges, behind bridge piers, in deep river pools and similar spots in the current. Present the bait anywhere between the surface and the bottom, depending on the method used and the local conditions.

The best bait

A favourite food of the brown trout is caddis fly larvae, but they also feed on other insects and small crustacea. Occasionally they will also eat small fish. Their food varies according to the waters they inhabit; in very cold waters containing little food, they have to make do largely with food that falls or lands on the surface.

Dry and wet flies are the most effective option for brown trout. Small spinners, spoons and wobblers, insects and sometimes baitfish can all be used as well. Worms may also snare them, but because this is not all that easy, you should only try it in waters where fly-fishing and spin fishing are not allowed.

The fly is the classic bait for brown trout.

Brown trout bite well on small spinners.

Lake Trout

Finger-length baitfish are always effective.

DE: Seeforelle, Lachsforelle,
FR: Truite de lac,
ES: Trucha lacustre,
NL: Forel,
SE: Insjööring,
PL: Tro jeziorowa

Distribution

Lake trout are found in all north-western and northern European coastal waters as well as the rivers that feed them. They also occur in the region of the Black Sea and White Sea, in Scandinavia, and in the British Isles. There are also populations in lakes in the Alps and their foothills.

Lake trout prefer cold, well oxygenated water that is as deep as possible. For this reason, they are most often encountered in mountain lakes, as these tend best to fulfil their requirements. They are found up to altitudes of around 2,000 m (78,000 ft). But lake trout also feel very much at home in rivers with a strong current. While the young fish like to stay out in open water, adults tend to live at the bottom and are territorial. They therefore require hideouts in the deep-water zones where they can lie in wait for their prey.

Lake trouts' spawning period depends on where they are living. Spawning takes place between September and December. As a rule, the fish begin migrating at the end of August to the upper reaches of the rivers that flow into their home waters, but this is not always the case. They look for places with a high oxygen level and a gravelly bottom. There, they dig spawning hollows into which each female lays up to 30,000 eggs, 5.0 to 5.5 mm in diameter. After spawning, the fish head back to the lakes.

Average lake trout specimens attain a length of between 40 to 80 cm and a weight of up to 5 kg. You will mostly find lake trout of this size in lakes where there is not much food. To grow really large, they need a wide range of food. If this is available, they can grow to 140 cm long and weigh

Lake Trout

When fishing in deeper areas, heavy spoons should be used.

up to 30 kg. So in fact they can grow to be larger than sea trout. Lake trout have considerable appetites and are therefore not always welcome in all waters.

If you want to catch lake trout in particular, it is best to try from April to May and the end of August to September. However, note that in late summer, especially, it is useless angling for them with a rod; you are far more likely to meet with success fishing from a boat using a trolling reel. This is because the fish are very deep down at this time, if they have not already begun their spawning migration.

During the rest of the year, a light or medium spinning rod is all you need. If the current is strong, however, it is better to use medium-weight tackle. Present the bait near the bottom: possible shelters such as sunken branches should be taken into account and are always good fishing spots.

Characteristics

Lake trout have a similar body shape to that of the brown trout. However, the flanks and the dorsal fin and tail fin are covered with black, x-shaped spots instead of red patches. They have a large head with powerful teeth and the typical adipose fin. The basic colour is very dark, but varies. This is because lake trout can adapt to the colour of the bottom, though only very slowly. Young lake trout and brown trout can only be distinguished from each other with difficulty, as they have the same red spots.

The best bait

Young lake trout feed on small invertebrates near the water surface and on plankton. Once they are mature, the adults' diet consists almost solely of fish, so the best way to catch them is by using baitfish. However, spoons also work very well.

Light spoons are better for shallow waters.

Sea Trout

Distribution

Just like their relatives, the lake trout, sea trout are found in the coastal waters of northern and north-western Europe and swim back up the rivers to breed. Their southern limit is Portugal, and to the north-east the White Sea marks the end of the waters they inhabit.

Sea trout inhabit coastal waters and prefer them to be cold and well oxygenated, although they are hardier than rainbow trout. The sea trout is considered the ancestral form of all European trout. Sea trout favour large, flowing waters which provide plenty of places to shelter. Overhanging vegetation, hollowed-out banks and other hiding places to a depth of 10 m are all suitable for sea trout. This predatory fish is active during the day. On reaching sexual maturity they occupy and defend their own territory. In some ways, their lifestyle and behaviour resemble those of the salmon, as sea trout also return to rivers in order to spawn.

Sea trout congregate in the brackish waters at river mouths as early as June or July and begin to swim upstream. During this time, the male develops a kype, or hooked lower jaw, as sea trout also engage in fierce fighting

Sea Trout

Characteristics

Sea trout, like other types of trout, have the ability to slowly change their colour to blend in with the bottom of their habitat. Their basic colouring is dark and blackish. The sides are lighter and have a large number of small, irregular black spots. Like other trout, sea trout have a torpedo-shaped body, powerful teeth, a large head and an adipose fin. The tail fin is nearly straight with barely any indentation.

with rivals during the spawning period, although they are less violent than salmon. Between October and May—the exact timing depends on where the fish live— each female lays as many as 10,000 eggs, 5 to 6 mm in diameter, in places which have a fast current and a gravelly bottom.

After reproducing, the parent fish rest up for some time before heading back to the sea. The young sea trout remain in fresh water for about two years, and migrate downstream for the first time when they have reached a length of around 15 cm.

Sea trout attain an average length of between 40 and 80 cm and weigh between 1 and 5 kg. Occasionally, a specimen may attain lengths of up to 110 cm and weigh 10 kg.

If you want to catch sea trout, try during the months of July and August. Use a medium-weight spinning rod or fly rod, and present the bait at a variety of depths. Places that provide shelter for the fish either above or below the water are the best. The best time is between the early hours of morning and late evening.

When fishing for sea trout, fairly large spinners are just the thing.

Colourful rubber fish can also be a good option.

The best bait

The natural diet of the sea trout includes insect larvae, small crustacea and fish, but their staples depend on their size. When choosing bait, you need to take into account how large the fish grow in the place you are going to be fishing. Wet and dry flies, as well as relatively large spinners, are the main options. However, spoons, casting spoons and redworms have all brought good results.

Skilful anglers can achieve catches like this on a regular basis.

Charr

DE: Seesaibling,
FR: Omble chevalier,
ES: Trucha alpina,
NL: Riddervis, beeksridder,
SE: Röding, fjällröding,
PL: Golec zwyczajny

Distribution

Charr are unevenly distributed throughout Europe. In Scandinavia, they are only to be found in the north and north-west; in Russia occasionally on the Finnish border and in the north. Charr also appear in alpine regions, i. e. in the foothills of the Alps, as well as in the northwest of Iceland. Charr are confined to the north and west of the British Isles.

The best bait

While young charr primarily eat plankton and small invertebrates, as the fish become older they increasingly move on to become bottom-feeders, feeding rapaciously on numerous types of aquatic fauna.

Consider using artificial flies and thin metal spoons as bait. Also worth trying are baitfish, maggots, and woodworms.

Charr are classified as the stationary form of the "wandering" charr (*Salvelinus alpinus*) and are found in various forms, all of which choose clear, deep lakes as their environment. Steep banks and gravel-covered bottoms are preferred by charr, although in practice the behaviour and characteristics of these fish differ from one lake to another. Therefore it is not always clear whether their occurrence represents different age groups or actually independent species of fish.

Salvelinus alpinus is a dwarf form of charr found only in high mountain lakes, which have a water temperature which never exceeds 10 °C (50 °F). Here they tend to remain in deep water.

Charr reproduce from October to March, the exact time depending upon each particular body of water. The female lays up to 6,000 eggs, 4 to 4.5 mm in diameter, on the gravel bottom near the shore. Depending upon the water temperature, the eggs may take more than 100 days to hatch. On average, charr of this species reach approximately

Characteristics

Charr have a torpedo-shaped body which becomes stockier with age, with a somewhat humped back. The back may vary in colour from dark blue-grey to blackish; the flanks are lighter or blue-grey. They are patterned with small, red or orange-coloured spots; however, these often appear to be lighter, because their effect is rather indistinct. The stomach is generally silver-white, but the males can take on a luminous red during spawning. Charr have an adipose fin; the front edges of the pelvic, pectoral and anal fins are white. The caudal fin is only indented in young fish.

15 to 20 cm in length and become sexually mature in two to three years.

The best time to catch charr is between May and June. You will want to use a leger rod or float rod with a sliding float, or possibly a light or medium-size deep-sea trawling rod. If possible, set your bait where the bottom of a stretch of water is elevated.

Speckled Trout

Speckled trout require cool water, high in oxygen, with quickly flowing sections. They tolerate lower pH and oxygen levels than the brown trout (*Salmo trutta fario*). Speckled trout tend to inhabit cold lakes, where they mass in large shoals in open water.

From October to March speckled trout reproduce in waters with strong currents. The female lays 2,000 eggs per kilo of body weight, each 4 mm across, into a spawning hollow. Finally, the eggs are churned into the gravel bottom by the

Other names: Aurora trout, brook charr, brook trout

DE: Bachsaibling, FR: Omble de fontaine, Saumon de fontaine, ES: Trucha de arroyo, NL: Bronforel, SE: Bäckröding, PL: Pstrąg r dlany

Distribution

Introduced from North America, speckled trout have spread in Europe through stocking. They are found in mountain regions like the Alps, the Pyrenees, the German low-mountain region, as well as in the Carpathian Mountains, Scotland and Scandinavia. They have since formed self-replicating stocks with varying success.

Characteristics

Speckled trout belong to the most vibrantly colourful of the freshwater fish: the dark, brown-green back is decorated with numerous light green to yellow spots, which flow together in the direction of the dorsal and caudal fins in a marbled effect. On the flanks there are often tiny red dots which have thin white and coarser blue borders, so that at first glance they seem only to be a single-coloured blue. Besides a large head and a very deep mouth opening, speckled trout have an adipose fin and a trim tail stem as well. The caudal fin is clearly indented; the front edges of the pelvic and anal fins are rimmed with white. Males develop an additional black stripe during the spawning period.

parents. Due to water temperatures of 5 °C (41 °F), it takes approximately 100 days for the eggs to hatch. The fry live off their yolk sacs for a good 40 days before they make the transition to actively feeding themselves. Speckled trout average 20 to 40 cm in length and weigh 250 g to 1 kg. In their native North America, prime specimens can weigh up to 5 kg.

The best season to find speckled trout is between April and September. Take a light to middle-heavy fly or spin fishing rod to purposefully pursue these fish. Bear in mind that speckled trout are not nearly so full of fight as charr or rainbow trout. The best fly to use depends upon which insects are naturally available where you are fishing.

The most enticing fly is the one that imitates the natural specimen.

The best bait

Insect and amphibian larvae, small crayfish, winged insects and invertebrates of all kinds form the main sources of food for the speckled trout. Larger specimens also pursue small fish and amphibians.

When selecting bait you have a wide range of choices, but the first to try out are dry and wet flies, preferably nymphs. Other possible alternatives are small spoons, spinners and wobblers, variations on artificial or natural insects and, in exceptional cases, worms are always worth a try.

Small spinners may also meet with success.

Rudd

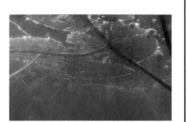

Rudd like to pass the time under water lilies.

DE: Rotfeder, FR: Rotengle, sergent, ES: Escardino, NL: Ruisvoorn, rietvoorn, SE: Sarv, PL: Wzdręga

Distribution

Rudd are widely distributed throughout Europe. In Scandinavia, they are confined to Denmark and the southern tip of Sweden and Finland. They occur neither in northern Russia, southern Turkey, southern Italy, extreme north-west France, nor in Scotland. Otherwise, they make their home all over Europe, except for the Peloponnese off the coast of Greece, where one finds the Greek rudd (Scardinius graecus) instead.

Where water lilies and reeds are not present, thick vegetation makes a good place to fish.

Rudd have a preference for water that is not too deep with lush vegetation; therefore they live mainly in still or slowly flowing bodies of water. They generally favour quiet bank areas or patches of reed and pond weed on the water surface. Only in winter do rudd withdraw into deeper regions. Rudd do not congregate in great numbers as roach do, but they gather in similar, although smaller, shoals. Rudd can tolerate low oxygen levels with ease; however, they are very sensitive to pollution. And because they are resistant to high salt levels, they can also be found in brackish water. In general, you can find rudd wherever the water temperature reaches at least 22 °C (71 °F) in the summer.

Rudd begin spawning in April and the spawning period lasts until about June. The exact duration depends upon prevailing weather conditions, because the fish require a minimum water temperature of 18 °C (64 °F) in order to reproduce. They spawn in small groups or in pairs in the underwater vegetation. As a result, the reddish but transparent eggs stick to the plants. Each female lays as many as 200,000 eggs of up to 1.5 mm in diameter. After hatching the fry still feed on their yolk sacs—it can take up to ten days before they are able to swim and find food for themselves.

Rudd

The chances of catching rudd are particularly good in shallow water near patches of reed.

An average rudd grows to be between 20 and 30 cm long, reaching a maximum of 45 cm in length and weighing up to 1 kg. These fish have a relatively long lifespan, and it is not unknown for them to reach an age of 19 years.

It is possible to catch rudd from spring until autumn, with your greatest chances of success in the summer months. The recommended approach is light float fishing or light legering, offering the bait in areas with dense aquatic vegetation. Good places to fish include spots near reeds and lots of underwater vegetation or near beds of water lilies, where you should fish from a middle depth up to the surface.

Characteristics

Rudd have a hump-like back and very flattened sides with brown-green colouring on the back, yellow-golden flanks and a white abdomen. All its fins are reddish to luminous red; the dorsal fin is distinctly behind the pelvic fin. The scales are large, forming a sharp keel between the pelvic fin and the anus. In particular, distinguishing features to be aware of are the rudd's small, upturned mouth and the yellow to gold-coloured, shiny eyes.

The best bait

Rudd feed primarily on parts of plants and new plant growth; however, they also eat plankton and small invertebrates.

Maggots, sweetcorn, and bread dough have proven to be among the best baits for this fish. Also, combining sweetcorn with a maggot is an extremely successful strategy. In addition to these baits, try insects of all kinds (depending upon the specific environment), various kinds of earthworms including small redworms or dungworms, casters and dry flies. Another option you might try is bread crust.

Sweetcorn is good bait for rudd.

Rudd can be very picky, but by offering a variety of baits there is always a good chance of a successful catch.

Catfish

DE: Wels, waller, FR: Silure glane, ES: Siluro, NL: Meerval, SE: Mal, PL: Sum

Distribution

Catfish were originally native to an area stretching from the Aral basin to eastern France, that is to the watershed of the Elbe river system. They were introduced into Great Britain about 100 years ago. Today, catfish are at home in nearly all of Europe through stocking although in some northern places (southern Sweden, for example) their numbers are decreasing rapidly. In contrast, there are particularly good stocks in Spain, Italy, France and Germany, as well as in Romania and Hungary.

Beating the catfish up from the bottom with catfish-wood.

Catfish seek out warmth and therefore prefer bodies of water which reach a temperature of at least 20 °C (68 °F) in the summer. Because they are not terribly particular regarding the water quality and oxygen levels, you come across catfish in just about every kind of still or quietly-flowing body of water. Strong currents do not trouble them either, so it is not surprising to come across catfish in larger rivers with very turbulent water, too. Because of this lack of sensitivity, catfish may even spend time in brackish water in delta areas.

To say that catfish are loners would not necessarily be correct. It is closer to the truth to say that catfish behaviour is dependent upon the type of water they inhabit and upon the local fish population. For example, catfish in a lake with a large number of other catfish tend to form small gangs and even to go on raids together. If their choice of suitable shelters is restricted then this is even more likely to be the case. Also, in bodies of water with smaller catfish stocks but limited hiding places, you are likely to encounter catfish together more often than alone.

Only in environments with small catfish stocks and sufficient cover—and assuming there is enough food present—do you find the catfish as loners, loyal to their location. Furthermore, if the natural food source is concentrated in one or only a few areas then catfish will,

again, form groups. By the way, the age distribution of the catfish does not matter; even really prime specimens live peacefully with many smaller members of their own species.

When they are not hunting, catfish spend their time in their

Catfish

shelters or even bury themselves in the lake or river bed, which is why they prefer a soft bottom to the body of water where they live—mud, for example.

In the same way, the time when these predatory fish hunt depends upon similar factors. The widely held belief that catfish are nocturnal is a fallacy. In bodies of water where there is lots of noise during the day—for example people swimming—which affects catfish adversely, then they will certainly be more likely to go on raids in the quiet hours. However, in remote

Catfish

Use a fixed float rig when fishing in strong currents over depressions.

The best bait

While young catfish eat typical bottom food such as worms, insect larvae, snails and small crayfish, adults of the species rarely show mercy to any animals. They eat fish, amphibians and crabs—not even small waterfowl or mammals are safe from its wide mouth.

The most successful choices of bait are fish and cuttlefish; above all, the use of eels has proven successful. But bundles of large lobworm, entrails, blood leeches and even spinners and wobblers are definitely worth deploying.

Cuttlefish are a proven catfish bait.

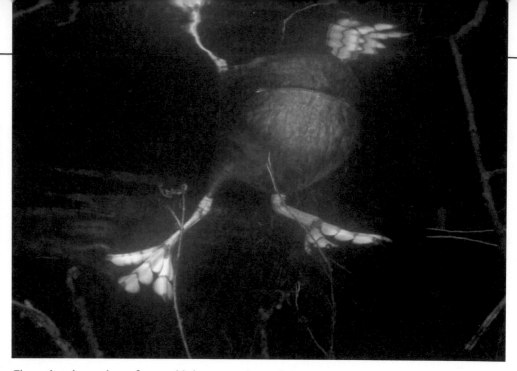

The swimming noises of water birds may make catfish aggressive.

lakes and rivers, they will hardly allow this time to go unused, as long as sufficient daytime prey are present. Catfish favour dawn and dusk above all other times for feeding.

Catfish recognise their prey by means of the weak electrical fields they emit, which the fish tune in to by using their electro-receptors. Their sense of hearing is also very well developed—the air bladder amplifies sound waves and transmits them to the inner ear. This comes about through a system of bones which are connected to one another. Catfish also have highly developed senses of touch, taste and smell.

Catfish require a water temperature of at least 18 °C (64 °F) in order to reproduce, which they do between May and June. They explore areas of shallow water for lush plant growth, where they spawn in pairs. The female lays as many as 480,000

yellowish eggs, that are 3.0 to 3.5 mm in diameter, in shallow holes or stuck to plants, roots or similar growth. After fertilization the eggs lose their colouration. Both parents

Fishing for catfish with eels: bait the eel just behind the head.

Catfish

keep watch over the eggs and often even guard the fry after they have hatched.

Young catfish grow very quickly and on average attain lengths of between 1 and 2 m. In fact, they never stop growing entirely, and some live to a ripe old age: specimens 80 years old have been known. Real giants of 3 m can weigh as much as 200 kg.

Catfish can be caught the whole year round; however, they bite particularly well after spawning, because they eat a great deal of food during that period. Light, short boat rods or heavy legering rods should be equipped with medium to heavy multiplier or stationary reels and braided lines. Good fishing locations are places that afford catfish with

shelter, for example sunken trees; vary your choice of bait offered on a braided leader according to the animals' biting behaviour. Using a catfish-wood to lure them by beating is helpful. You should try to avoid the use of a landing hook, called a gaff, when landing catfish. Instead, try to treat a catfish gently by wearing gloves and holding it firmly by the protruding lower jaw.

What a catch! Catfish can grow to over 2 m long.

Fishing with a friend is double the fun and may bring double the results.

Characteristics

Catfish are very large, elongated fish. They are round in the front in cross section, but the sides flatten out behind the anus. The back is dark green or brown to blackish, while the flanks are lighter and covered with dark marbling. The head is very broad and flat with tiny eyes. Catfish have a large mouth full of numerous tiny teeth, which become crooked towards the back. They sport two long barbels (fleshy filaments) on their upper lip and four more on the underside of the head. They have no scales, and have a very short back fin, as well as a small caudal fin. The anal fin and tail are quite extended.

Pike-perch

Other names: Zander

DE: Zander, FR: Sandre, ES: Lucioperca, NL: Snoekbaars, SE: Gös, PL: Sandacz

Distribution

The original western distribution border of pike-perch was the watersheds of the Elbe and Danube rivers; however, currently their range reaches France, Spain and Great Britain, which was achieved through stocking. They are evenly distributed throughout central Europe, including the regions of the Baltic Sea and the Kiel Canal which have a lower salt concentration, as well as to the Aral basin in the east.

The bodies of water which the pike-perch inhabit include lakes, rivers, canals and reservoirs, as long as the food supply is rich enough and the waters flow relatively slowly. Because these fish shun the light, they prefer bodies of water where the water is not too clear; they feel particularly comfortable in murky lakes in summer, for example. Pike-perch prefer deep waters with a solid

74

Pike-perch

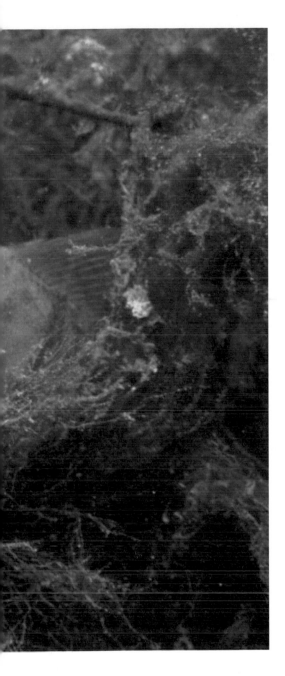

Double-tailed twisters wobble in a manner particularly seductive for pike-perch.

live in small shoals there and move around quite a lot. Pike-perch do not seek out sheltered spots as frequently as other predatory fish. Instead, they like to hunt in open waters, again, in small shoals more often than singly. However, if pike-perch are not travelling within the body of water they inhabit, they prefer roots, stones or deep grooves to serve as their base.

Pike-perch can be active during the day or they can be nocturnal; exactly when they are most active depends upon their environmental circumstances. Basically, if the fish they prey on prefer to spend their time in shallow sections of water, the pike-perch will first begin feeding at dusk. During the day they are not usually to be found near the shore nor in other zones of shallow water.

During the spawning period, though, things are a little different. Spawning occurs between April and June; the exact timing depends upon the water temperature, because pike-perch require at least 10 °C (50 °F) before they will reproduce. They are very demanding concerning the choice of an ideal spawning location: the male will choose only an area of shallow water near the bank which has a depth of about 1.5 m and a clean bottom. Once he has found a suitable place, the male cleans up the spawning substrate on hand—for example, roots—and forms it into a hole. The female lays over 300,000 eggs of 1

The best bait

Adult pike-perch feed exclusively on small fish, while the young of the species at first eat animal plankton and insect larvae.

When you are fishing for pike-perch, always give first preference to baitfish; but do bear in mind that these animals can eat only relatively small fish. Twisters and small rubber fish have also proven to be very good bait choices. However, fish pieces, wobblers, lobworms and small spinners can also bring success.

When fishing for pike-perch rubber fish need to be near the bottom.

earth bottom and little underwater vegetation.

Nevertheless, they are also to be found in bodies of water that are not so murky. In that case it will most likely be a very deep lake, as they withdraw into water deeper than 5 m. In an ideal environment, that is, in a murky body of water, the pike-perch tend to be found at depths of 2 to 3 m. As a rule, they

The characteristic long teeth of the pike-perch are easy to recognise.

to 1.5 mm in diameter. Depending upon the spawning situation the eggs are laid either in one large or in several clumps, which are interwoven with the nesting material. The fry hatch approximately ten days later. Until then the brood is guarded by the male, who gently fans fresh water into the nest with his pectoral fin.

Characteristics

The back of the pike-perch is grey-green in colour and equipped with blackish, washed-out bands. The flanks are decorated in light grey, the abdomen in white. The spindle-shaped body is equipped with small, raw comb-like scales; the back is more prominently curved than the stomach. The jaw of the forward-facing and deep-cutting mouth is full of many small teeth and a few large ones much like fangs, the so-called dog's teeth. The anal, caudal and dorsal fins are covered with dark points, or to be precise, spots. On the gill cover the pike-perch bears a small, inconspicuous barb; its frontal dorsal fin is equipped with rays of hard spines.

During the spawning phase, pike-perch do not eat and for up to two weeks afterwards they stay in the shallow water. Apparently, females are particularly delicate, as they sometimes die after spawning.

Pike-perch reach an average length of 40 to 70 cm; however, given an abundant food supply they can grow to a length of 1.3 m and weigh up to 15 kg.

You can fish for pike-perch from August into the winter months. However, late summer and autumn have proven to be the most favourable times. Angle with a light to heavy legering rods or a spin rod, depending upon the condition of the currents and the size of bait you intend to use. With rubber worms, use a somewhat stiffer rod with tip action.

Pike-perch

When looking for an ideal place to fish, one should at first look for spots where the pike-perch may be, for example, behind groynes, at the edges of the current, or near sunken tree limbs or roots. When you have found a likely-looking area, of course, that is no guarantee that pike-perch also hunt there, so you should always fish a wider area. Particularly good areas to angle for pike-perch are always locations where shallow hunting zones and deep standing water lie quite near to one another.

Pike-perch generally bite at more specific times during the day than most other predatory fish—outside of their hunting groups they will only seldom bite under most conditions. Only in very murky bodies of water can they be counted on to bite throughout the day.

When legering, place the bait immediately above the bottom. Spin fishing requires a deep and slow introduction of the bait. In bodies of water where pike are also present, definitely use a steel leader.

Spin fishing at dusk gives a good chance of a bite.

Lead the artificial bait with irregular movements.

Grayling

Other names: Umber

DE: Äsche, FR: Ombre,
ES: Tímalo, NL: Vlagzalm,
SE: Harr, PL: Lipie

Distribution

Grayling inhabit the region extending from England across to Denmark, central Sweden and Lapland ending at the White Sea. In central Europe grayling are to be found from eastern France to the alpine regions of northern Italy. Grayling are not present in the Mediterranean, northern Scandinavia, Ireland and Scotland.

Nymphs are the classic grayling bait.

Grayling demonstrate a preference for cool, oxygen-rich and rather deep water and therefore are present generally only in rivers and large streams. In northern Europe they occasionally are to be found in clear lakes, as well. Grayling are less sensitive than brook trout, for example, to short-term elevations in temperature up to 25 °C (77 °F), whereas a water temperature under 4 °C (39 °F) is problematic for them. Grayling are very sensitive to pollution in the water. They prefer to spend their time in waters in where quick-flowing and quiet areas alternate and where the bottom is solid. Here they usually can be found near the edge of deep holes or in

Grayling

Characteristics

Grayling have rather small scales, which appear more hexagonal than round, and a small, pointed head with a downward-turned mouth (the upper jaw extends further than the lower one). The back is a blue-grey colour, while flanks and abdomen have a silver-white colouration. The body is like that of a trout; an adipose fin is also present. Small back spots, edged with white, are distributed on the front half of the body on the sides. The caudal fin is clearly notched. The dorsal fin is noticeably larger on the males than on the females and distinctly sail-like. Overall, it has rather large and colourful bands; the pelvic fins are most often reddish coloured.

the midst of underwater vegetation, where the fish stay together in small groups and lie in wait for potential prey to swim by.

The spawning period of the grayling begins in March and lasts into June. In water approximately 50 cm deep the female makes a hole and in it lays as many as 10,000 eggs with a diameter if 3.2 to 4 mm. After the fertilization, the spawn are mixed in with the gravel bottom.

An average grayling specimen is 30 to 50 cm long and weighs between 250 g and 1.5 kg when fully grown, though prime examples measuring up to 60 cm and weighing 2.5 kg have been recorded.

Between June and November, particularly directly after the spawning period and into September, is the best time to fish for grayling. Use light or medium-weight tackle with a fly rod, depending upon your choice of bait. If this is not successful, you may wish to try legering with light tackle as an alternative. After the spawning, and also in winter, you can achieve rather good catches with spoons or worms offered near the bottom, because grayling not only feed on flies at the surface, but also on bottom-dwelling creatures.

In waters that are frequently fished, grayling stock inevitably decrease rapidly, because the females of this species become sexually mature much later than the males, but are more likely to bite and be taken by the angler.

Small spinners result in success when fishing for grayling.

The best bait

When grayling are in deep waters, they feed on insect larvae and small crayfish. However, they will also feed on insects on the water surface. Larger specimens are also known to occasionally catch a small fish.

The best way to convince graylings to bite is with insects and artificial flies. Here the dry flies, in particular, have proven to be successful quite often. Alternatively, you can try your luck with small spoons and worms.

Tench

DE: Schleie, FR: Tanche, aiguillons,
ES: Tenca, NL: Zeelt,
SE: Lindare, sutare, PL: Lin

Distribution

Tench can be found in almost all of Europe to the Ural Mountains. Its distribution in the Mediterranean is limited, and it is definitely absent from the coastal areas near Slovenia, Turkey and Corsica. In Scandinavia tench are only found in Denmark and in the south of Sweden and Finland. They inhabit the northern part of the Iberian Peninsula and Great Britain but do not range as far north as Scotland.

The tench is a pure bottom fish, which means they spend their time only near the bottom. They prefer to inhabit still waters which are rich in vegetation and have a muddy substrate, so they are primarily found in shallow, warm lakes with a fairly low concentration of oxygen. However, the tench is rather adaptable, and they also can be found in the brackish water of the Baltic Sea, or at altitudes of ap-

Tench

proximately 1,600 m. In flowing waters they only feel comfortable where they find their preferred environment; therefore, older branches of rivers are most likely to have good tench stock.

The tench is a fish which becomes active at dusk. Lush plant growth in which they can hide themselves during the day is very important for their sense of well-being.

In very hot summers, a time in which muddy, shallow waters in particular often contain little oxygen, the tench falls into a kind of summer trance. It slays in its hideout and barely moves; its exchange of oxygen is thereby reduced to an absolute minimum, and it doesn't eat. As soon as the water conditions make a turn for the better again, the fish returns to its normal lifestyle.

Just how adaptable the tench really is becomes clear in the winter, because then also a dangerous lack of oxygen can occur quickly in its preferred environment. Especially shallow lakes may freeze quickly in a hard winter. In this case, the tench simply bury themselves in the muddy bottom and remain there in a winter trance until more favourable conditions predominate again. In waters with less extreme conditions, the fish spend the winter in deeper waters. There the fish come together in small groups, even though they tend to be loners the rest of the year.

For the tench, the exact timing of spawning is strongly dependent upon its environment, because it requires a water temperature of 18 to 20 °C (64 to 68 °F) in order to spawn. Most of the time the animals reproduce from May to July. However, depending upon weather conditions, it may take place as early as April or even continue into August. Male tenches have a spawning rash on their head and back

Fresh worms are particularly good for catching tench.

The best bait

Tenches' natural food consists of all kinds of small animals that live on the bottom and soft plant parts. When choosing bait there are numerous possibilities. Corn, dungworms and maggots (big and small—the dyed maggots called pinkies, as well) have proven to be outstanding bait.

As alternatives, the use of grain, small earthworms or water snails can be recommended; lobworms, bread, dough, cheese and boilies may also lead to fine catches.

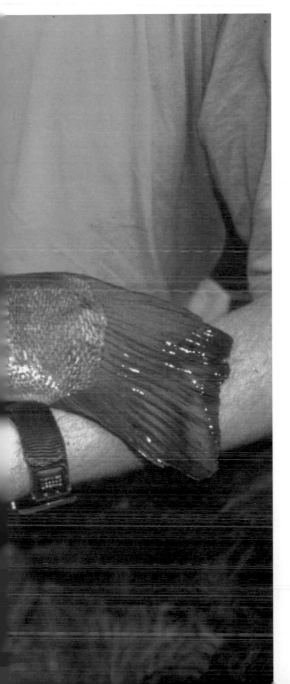

Living bait is kept fresh in spacious containers.

Tench

Characteristics

The tench has a very strong build, small scales and a thick, slimy skin. Their backs are dark brown to olive in colouring; the sides are olive-green and the abdomen yellow. In the corners of the short mouth, which is located at the front of the head (i. e. the jaws are of equal length), it has two very short barbels. The high and strong root of its tail flows into a straight, barely indented fin. Overall, the fins are rather dark and rounded. Male tenches have extended pelvic fins, which are thickened on the second ray.

Completely unveiled: portait of the head of a tench.

during this time. The fish gather together in small groups and look for bank areas with substantial plant growth, where each female may lay up to 300,000 green-yellow to orange-coloured eggs. With a diameter of less than 1 mm they are rather small, and they stick to the water plants. It can take 1 to 2 weeks until all the eggs are laid, because the tench spawns in several phases.

The young fish hatch after just three or four days, but are not yet able to swim. To prevent themselves from sinking into the mire, in which they wouldn't have any chance of survival, they attach themselves at first for several days to the water plants until they are able to swim. They possess several sticky glands for this purpose; one finds similar characteristics in fish species which live in bodies of water with soft bottoms.

Tench

Most tench reach lengths between 20 and 40 cm, and they weigh 500 g to 1.5 kg. The maximum size is 70 cm, weighing up to 10 kg.

Precise determination of the primary fishing season is not possible, because the tench is dependent upon weather conditions and the waters it inhabits. As a rule, however, one can say that the tench bites well in the months of March and April and then again starting in July on into October. In very shallow waters the season may, however, begin somewhat earlier, and because the water temperature increases more quickly and leads to an earlier spawning period, it is quite possible that the fish will already bite again in May. The angler should therefore study the water environment of the target fish population and take into account both the spawning time as well as the possible summer and winter trances.

When you intend to fish for tench, it is recommended to groundbait at your selected fishing spot ahead of time. Ideal places such as banks with lots of reeds, vegetation or water lilies, are promising. When legering or float fishing, with light to medium tackle, you should offer your bait close to but not directly on the bottom.

With an electronic bite indicator, the patient waiting becomes child's play.

Natural and reed-covered waters are likely spots to make a good catch.

Wolffish

DE: Seewolf,
FR: Loup de mer,
ES: Lobo,
NL: Zeewolf,
SE: Havskatt,
PL: Zębacz pospolity

Distribution

Wolffish inhabit the north Atlantic coast of Norway, the north Atlantic islands and Iceland. One finds it likewise in Kattegat on the north-east coast of Scotland and less frequently in the western part of the North Sea. It is not found in the Mediterranean.

Characteristics

The striped wolffish is a fish with an elongated body and large head. Its basic colour is usually green-greyish, though individual specimens may also have almost black or reddish colouring. Ten to fifteen dark stripes adorn it from the dorsal fin upward as well. Its broad, round mouth is quite full of massive teeth. The dorsal and anal fin edges do not grow together with the caudal fin. It has tiny scales which are deeply embedded in the skin.

The striped wolffish is a confirmed bottom dweller that prefers a hard, rocky bottom in its natural environment, which may also be covered with seaweed. However, one also finds the wolffish from time to time on a sandy or muddy floor. Depending upon the environment, this loner fish feels comfortable in depths from approximately 20 to 500

Wolffish

The crab is a hard but good bait for wolffish.

metres. Because the wolffish gets its nourishment from hard-shelled invertebrates, it has a very powerful set of teeth at its disposal. These become worn out fairly quickly, however, and are therefore replaced every year in the winter.

The season of reproduction for the wolffish lies between October and January, but may also extend into February in some regions. The eggs of the wolffish are 5 to 6 mm large, and each female lays up to 25,000 eggs; the exact number varies according to the size of the female. Spawning occurs over the ocean floor, where the eggs are laid in balls. There, they will be guarded by the males until the young fish hatch after approximately eight weeks. During this period, the male wolffish barely eats. After

Any angler should be tremendously pleased with such a catch.

living for a quarter of a year off of their yolk sack, the small wolffish live at first in open water, switching to the typical bottom dweller lifestyle only when they are about 5 cm in length.

On average, the striped wolffish reaches a length of 60 to 80 cm and weighs about 3 to 4 kg; the maximum length of this fish is 150 cm and it can weigh over 20 kg.

The most favourable time for fishing this species is between March and May. It is preferable to fish in deep areas with stony bottoms. You can also give shallower areas, such as bays, a try on occasion in the summer. One should preferably use a stable boat rod with a multiplier reel which is equipped with a woven line. It is best to bait on or just above the bottom, and a gaff is a necessity to land these fish.

If the cuttlefish are too big, cut them in half.

The best bait

In its natural environment the diet of the wolffish includes mussels, crabs, crayfish and sea urchins.

A particularly efficient bait for wolffish is a small sack which is filled with mussels and attached to the hook. Also promising are starfish, whole crabs, cuttlefish and fish pieces.

Garfish

Other names: Hornpike

DE: Hornhecht, Grünknochen

F: Orphie, ES: Agulla, aguja, NL: Geep,

SE: Näbbgädda,

PL: Belona

Distribution

Garfish are to be found in the Atlantic and in the North Sea along the Norwegian coast, around the British Isles to Iceland. They also occur around the Danish coast as well and in the Baltic Sea.

Characteristics

The very long and trim body of the garfish is blue-green on its back; the flanks are silvery and shiny and its abdomen is coloured white. It has a very long, beak-shaped jaw, although the lower jaw is longer than the upper one. Its mouth contains numerous fine, pointed teeth. The dorsal and anal fins are opposite each other and only a small distance away from the caudal fin. All the fins on this fish are supported by soft rays.

Garfish are fish which live in swarms and in open water, where they spend most of their time just under the surface. They are outstanding swimmers and, starting in the spring, undertake far-reaching tours to the coastal areas of Europe. Only in cold seasons do these fish spend time at deeper levels of water.

Between May and June, depending upon when the animals reach the shallow water zone, the garfish reproduces. The number of eggs produced varies with the size of the female, and it is assumed that these fish even spawn several times each year. Between 1,000 and 35,000 eggs of circa 3.0 to 3.5 mm in diameter are produced in portions of 60 to 80 eggs on long, sticky strings. After the spawning process, the parent fish move around in order to prey on other fish in swarms. The diurnal predatory fish hunt on sight and cover long distances when searching for food.

Garfish

examples can become 90 cm long and weigh up to 1.3 kg. Garfish which are longer than 70 cm are not common, however.

The best time to catch garfish is from May to June, that is, directly after spawning. Most frequently one can outwit them with a float fishing rod, but fly or spin rods also have their moments. In any case, light tackle is completely adequate in order to pursue fish near the surface. When spin fishing, the bait should be placed rapidly. Garfish most often bite only when the sun is shining and the water completely clear. Good fishing spots are bridges, harbours and piers, although one should give preference to areas with stronger currents. At very shallow locations, it is advisable to don waders and go directly into the water.

With small, thin rubber bait, one has a good chance of catching garfish.

The best bait

As young animals the garfish eat small plankton; however, with advancing age they tend to switch over to crayfish, shrimp and small fish. The top baits are small pieces of fish and small spinners, but thin spoons and colourful streamers also give you good chances of achieving a fine catch.

After about four weeks the fry hatch; however, their lower jaw does not yet protrude. The beak-like snout forms only over time and reaches a length of approximately 12 cm. Garfish grow very quickly and as a rule are already approximately 20 cm long at one year of age. On average, they reach a length of 40 to 50 cm; prime

The movement of small spinners seduce the garfish into biting.

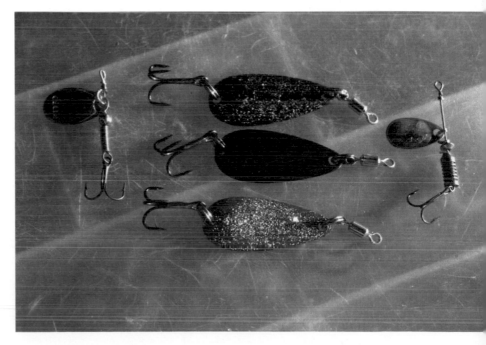

Tusk

Other names:
Torsk, moonfish

DE: Lumb, ES: Brosmio,
FR: Brosme, assiette,
NL: Lom, SE: Lumb, brosme,
PL: Brosma

Distribution

In the north Atlantic, the tusk is widely distributed all the way from the Norwegian coast to eastern and northern Great Britain and on to Iceland.

One finds the tusk at depths from around 50 to 1,000 m; however, it prefers to spend its time in areas between 150 and 500 meters deep near the bottom. It lives as a loner or in small swarms and prefers rough, stony or gravel-covered floors. However, one can also find it above muddy floors. As a rule, it will spend its time far from the shore and requires a water temperature between 4 and 10 °C (39 to 50 °F) in order to really feel comfortable.

The tusk spawns from April to July at depths of 40 to 400 m, although the most common band is around 100 to 200 m. Its most important spawning area lies between Scotland and Iceland: tusks reproduce in open water. In accordance with its other habits, it will be more of an exception when spawning takes place near the coast.

Each female lays approximately 2 to 3 million eggs 1.4 mm in size, which are carried away by the current. The young animals, which hatch after ten days, live in open waters for a period of about one and a half years. Only then do they switch to the life of a bottom-dweller.

The tusk reaches an average length of 90 cm and can weigh up to 10 kg. Prime specimens of 120 cm and 30 kg weight are less commonly caught but do, indeed, exist. This fish lives a rather long time; animals up to an age of 20 years are known.

Tusk

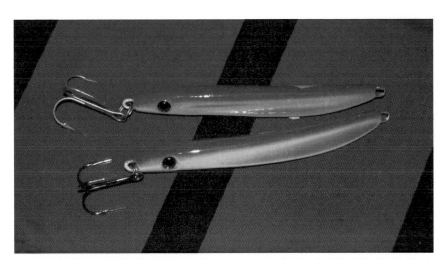

Pirks are particularly effective bait for catching tusk.

Fishing from a boat is the best way to target tusk.

The tusk can be hooked during the entire year. It bites best during the time directly after spawning and into August. Depending upon the spawning area, one can outwit it there in depths of between 50 and 200 m. When looking for a fishing spot, favour areas with rocky bottoms, where the tusk likes to conceal itself. Because of the depth of the water—and because this fish proves to be a fighter when reeling it in—heavy tackle is necessary: short, strong boat rods, large multiplier reels with strong lines and heavy sinkers. In the cold seasons the tusk moves to still deeper waters; on the average, you should take a depth of 300 to 400 m into consideration. Baits should be offered on or just above the bottom.

The best bait

The tusk's natural diet consists of fish, crayfish and mussels. Logical choices of bait include large chunks of fish (in particular herring), large shrimp and heavy pirks.

You will need heavy pirks to position the bait at the correct depth.

Characteristics

The colouration of this fish varies from dark red to greenish-brown on its back to a light, palish yellow shade on its abdomen. Young animals also have six yellow, diagonal bands on their flanks. Its long dorsal and anal fin is edged with white and extends almost to the caudal fin. Its thick, slimy skin is equipped with very small scales. The tusk does not have any barbels on its snout, but may occasionally have them on its chin.

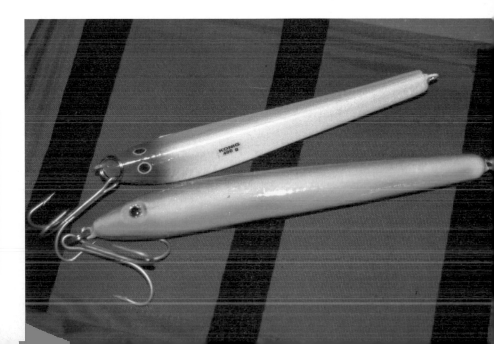

Thick-lipped Mullet

DE: Meeräsche,
FR: Mulet à grosses lèvres,
ES: Lisa, NL: Harder,
SE: Multe, PL: Chelon
grubowargi

Distribution

The thick-lipped mullet inhabits the coasts of the Mediterranean Sea and the Atlantic Ocean to Norway. One will also find the mullet around Ireland and Great Britain. In the summertime it temporarily visits the North Sea, and one comes across it in the mild Gulf Stream region in the southwest of Europe somewhat frequently. Its close relative, the thin-lipped mullet (Liza ramada) has a nearly identical distribution area, but is much more frequently represented in the Mediterranean region and is missing in the British Isles.

The thick-lipped mullet lives in swarms in tropical to moderate waters and appears in coastal areas as well as in brackish water. In the summertime, when the temperature rises, it likes to trek in a northern direction. Very frequently the mullet spends its time near the bottom, where it is apparently constantly busy with the search for food. This makes some sense when one considers that the mullet feeds largely on algae, and must scour stones that can be found under water to find it. Mullets suck in organic bottom deposits and plant parts and filter these with the aid of its long gill-trap process. They have a particularly muscular stomach and a very long intestine.

In the warm seasons you will also comes across these fish in open waters as well as near the surface. They are, for example, regular summer guests along the coast of the North Sea and particularly like to spend their time in the harbours. The same is true for the related thin-lipped mullet, which patrols the harbours in great swarms in summer.

In general, the thick-lipped mullet reproduces in Europe from February to June. Further northwest, however, for example in the English

Thick-lipped Mullet

Characteristics

The thick-lipped mullet has a broad head and two short dorsal fins which are quite far apart from one another. The first dorsal fin is equipped with four thorn-rays; the body is covered with large scales. Its noticeable upper lip is approximately as thick as the diameter of its pupil; really large mullets, in addition, have horny nodules on the underside of their mouth.

Channel and near the coast of Ireland, it spawns only between July and August. The female simply releases her eggs in open waters, where she—exactly like the larva later on—floats with the current.

Thick-lipped mullets reach a maximum weight of 4.5 kg and a length of 75 cm, and reach an age of around 25 years. They reach sexual maturity at approximately half their maximum size at the age of four.

The time following reproduction is particularly favourable for catching the mullet. Still, one should take into consideration the fact that this is a so-called "fair-weather fish", meaning that the worse the weather conditions become, the slimmer your chances of catching the thick-lipped mullet. Anyone who just can't resist and must fish with a strong wind should look for well-protected locations in order to avoid going home empty-handed.

Some people still maintain that it is very difficult to purposely fish for mullets; however, this is only partially true. It's admittedly true that this fish can be categorised as shy; however, this applies primarily to fishing by sight. Mullets see the angler, after all, just as quickly as she or he glimpses the fish. Still, you should be able to outwit them anywhere where a lot of potential food is present, because they are rather ravenous.

With light tackle, with a floater or a water ball, fine line and small hooks, set your bait between the central water and the surface. Especially important is the feeding; here one should proceed like with many fresh water fish and regularly feed them. At fishing spots where the landing could be difficult (e.g. in harbours), a swim feeder is a great help.

Small pieces of fish are always a delicacy for mullets.

The best bait

The primary food of the thick-lipped mullet consists of plankton organisms (e. g. algae), snails and other invertebrates. They also consume plant matter.

Dough which includes fish-meal is an excellent bait, or bread crumbs can be recommended. As alternatives, maggots and very small pieces of fish or flies are suitable.

Bread crumbs and dough are readily available forms of bait.

Herring

Other names:
Stroemling, yawling
DE: Hering,
FR: Hareng,
ES: Arenque,
NL: Haring, toter,
SE: Sill, strömming,
PL: led

Distribution

Herring primarily live in the north Atlantic, where they inhabit all the coasts surrounding the British Isles and the entire Scandinavian region. In addition, they range from the Bay of Biscay to the North Sea and on to the White Sea. In the Baltic the dwarf form of herring are known as stroemling. There are no herring in the Mediterranean Sea.

With shimmering little flags, herring pasternoster rigs tempt the fish to bite.

Herring live in open waters at a depth of up to 200 m and form giant shoals, which often comprise several tonnes of fish. During the day they remain in deeper water, rising to the surface at night to pursue their food source. Herring hunt by sight and are very adaptable. If food supplies are restricted, they can adapt to nourishing themselves entirely with plankton. In winter, herring barely eat anything at all and their growth is greatly retarded.

Herrings have an acute sense of hearing and also have the ability to react quickly, which they need in order to flee, as they are an important prey of numerous other fish species.

It is practically impossible to give complete information about the time span of their spawning period, because this depends upon the individual race or subspecies of herring and their geographic surroundings. In the Baltic, for example, herring spawn in the spring, while in the North Sea they spawn in the autumn.

Before spawning herring generally look for an area between the coast and deeper waters with a temperature of 5 to 7 °C (41 to 45 °F) and a depth of about 50 m, where eggs and semen are released into the open water. Each female produces 20,000 to 50,000 eggs of up to 1.5 mm in size. After fertilization

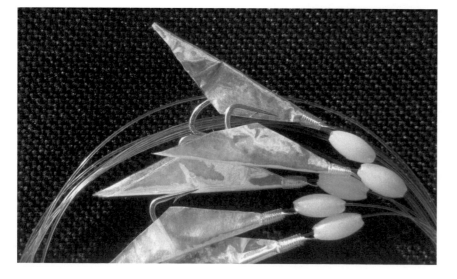

Herring

Characteristics

The back of the herring has a green-blue colour; the flanks and abdomen have a characteristic mother-of-pearl, silvery sheen. They have large scales and smooth gill covers. Herring have neither an adipose fin nor a lateral line; and the dorsal and anal fins are relatively small.

Bare hooks on paternoster tackle are effective for herring.

The best bait

Herring feed on swimming fish fry, tiny crustacea, molluscs and krill. They are best caught with bare hooks on paternoster tackle (i. e. short hook-lengths appended to the main line, with the weight fixed at the extreme end) or feather traces, bare hooks decorated with small, shimmering wings.

the eggs sink and stick to algae or stones.

Herring grow to a length of about 25 to 30 cm and an average weight of approximately 500 g. Their maximum length is 50 cm, weighing as much as 5 kg.

On the open sea you can fish for herring the whole year round; in coastal regions the best success is to be expected between March and May (particularly in the North Sea and the Baltic Sea). Locations featuring steep banks, such as bridges, ship docks or quay walls are especially promising fishing spots. With light rods, small fixed-spool reels and monofilament line that is not too thick you will be well equipped. Offer the bait at a variety of depths, depending upon the time of day.

Conger Eel

DE: Meeraal,
FR: Congre, anguille de
mer, ES: Congrio, negrillo,
congre, NL: Kongeraal,
zeepaling, SE: Havsål,
PL: Konger

Distribution

*Conger eel inhabit the
north-eastern coast of the
Atlantic from the south of
Norway around the British
Isles to western Africa. They
are also frequently found in
the Mediterranean.*

*Match the size of the bait to
the expected catch by cutting
the baitfish to a suitable size.*

Characteristics

*Conger eel are very similar
in shape to the river eel.
Their dark backs and the
white to yellowish abdo-
mens are nearly identical.
But in contrast to the river
eel, the conger has a longer
dorsal fin that is positioned
opposite the pectoral fin.
Conger eel have no scales;
their upper jaw is longer
than the lower jaw.*

Conger eel prefer to inhabit coastal areas with a solid bottom which offers good possibilities for cover, for example, cracks in the rocks, wrecks or caves. They are to be found at depths of up to 100 m; the older the eel, the further removed from the coast it will spend its time. Conger eel are nocturnal and predatory fish.

Conger eel have a reproductive season that extends between June and September; for this purpose they head for their spawning grounds off the Atlantic coast of Portugal and in the Mediterranean. Females each produce 3 to 8 million eggs; both the male and female parents die after the reproductive act. Once hatched, just like the river eel, the fry take on a flat form that looks much like a leaf. After one or two years spent in open water at a depth of up to 200 m, they metamorphose into the typical eel shape and move to shallower water areas near the coast.

Conger eel grow very quickly and reach an average size of 100 to 150 cm, although the males seldom grow

Conger Eel

Slim sardines attract larger conger eels.

beyond 100 cm. At this size congers weigh between 8 and 15 kg; really prime examples have been known to grow to 3 m in length and weigh up to 110 kg.

The best time to fish for conger eels is between June and October. When boat fishing, you need heavy boat rods with large multiplier reels, which should be equipped with braided line. For shore fishing leger rods are called for, they too need to be heavy models with a fixed-spool

reel or multiplier reel. In both cases, use a steel leader and strong hooks; a gaff is extremely helpful when it comes to landing conger eel. Present the bait near the sea bed and preferably choose a fishing spot where rocks or other ostacles offer the eels hiding places. However, you will experience the greatest success catching conger eel during the night, when they are out looking for their own prey. If there is a careful nibble don't react immediately, because the conger eel does not always completely swallow the bait immediately. Better to give a little line first, sink the tip of your rod a little—but don't wait too long! Once an eel retreats to its hiding place with its booty, reeling it in will be a difficult undertaking.

The best bait

Conger eels are primarily caught with baitfish; small cod, herring and mackerel make the best bait. Their natural food is mostly comprised of fish. But because conger eel supplement their diet with cuttlefish and crabs, using pieces of cuttlefish as bait has also proven effective.

Cuttlefish make good bait for large conger eels.

Sea Bass

Other names:
King of the mullets, white salmon, sea perch
DE: Wolfsbarsch, Seebarsch,
FR: Bar, ES: Lubina,
NL: Zeebaars, SE: Havsab-
borre, PL: Labraks

Distribution

Sea bass live in the Atlantic off the south and south-west coasts of the British Isles, France, Spain and Portugal. In the Mediter-ranean region they are found as far east as the Balkans. In summer, sea bass move into the North Sea as far up as the coast of southern Norway.

Sea bass are found primarily in coastal waters, because that is their preferred location. However, the sea bass also feels quite at home in estuaries and in the lower reaches of rivers. If you do encounter them out in the open sea, they will be near reefs or shipwrecks, because they need places where they can take cover; even in coastal regions they prefer a rocky sea bed.

Young sea bass form schools or even large shoals; in contrast, the older specimens are less social and are more likely to appear alone. Sea bass are predatory fish which are active at dusk and during the night. They like to seek their prey as the tide begins to run toward the shore, concentrating on places with sandy bottoms.

Sea bass reproduce between January and June; the exact timing depends upon their environment. Off the British Isles sea bass spawn in late spring and early summer, for example. Sea bass gather in small groups to spawn. The transparent eggs have a diameter from circa 1.2 to 1.3 mm and are laid in open water, where they are carried away by the current, because they are not sticky.

The time it takes for the fry to hatch depends upon the water temperature; at 13 °C (55 °F), for example, it takes almost five days, whereas at around 16 °C (61 °F) the

Sea Bass

Characteristics

Sea bass have large, silvery scales and a prominent black spot on their gill covers, which have two strong barbs on the back edge. Both dorsal fins are approximately the same length and are separated from one another. Young animals have a pattern of dark spots on their upper body.

Feathered spoons are always a good choice when hunting sea bass.

fry only need approximately two and a half days until they hatch. Sea bass average about 50 cm long. It used to be commonly assumed that they could reach a maximum length of 80 cm and a weight of 5 to 7 kg; however, more recently prime specimens of 103 cm, which weigh up to 12 kg, have been recorded.

Fishing for sea bass is worth your while from spring through the late autumn. It is best to fish where there are strong currents as opposed to a completely calm, or, for that matter, a very stormy sea. Fishing at

From a boat, you can use colourful jigs quite effectively.

the onset of dusk and through the night pays dividends; during the day it's only worth a try in overcast weather and poor light conditions. Shallow sections of beach should also be fished, because sea bass go there in search of food. It is a good idea to find out at ebb tide where sea bass could feed later.

In addition, you can determine the kind of food naturally available for the sea bass and tailor your choice of bait accordingly. Spin fishing, float fishing, surf casting and legering (also from a boat) are suitable fishing methods; with medium tackle you cannot go wrong in most circumstances.

The best bait

Sea bass eat fish and shrimp; therefore strips of mackerel, crab meat and shrimp should be your first choices for bait. When it comes to the question of artificial bait, twisters and rubber fish are to be recommended, as are blinkers and wobblers.

Wobblers are good bait near rocky coasts.

Grey Gurnard

DE: Knurrhahn,
FR: Grondin gris,
ES: Perlón,
NL: Grauwe poon,
SE: Knot, gnoding, knorr-
hane, PL: Kurek szary

Distribution

Grey gurnards are native to almost all European coasts, including those of the Mediterranean Sea. Around the British Isles and the eastern part of the North Sea they are seen particularly often. In the Baltic, however, they inhabit the western reaches only rarely. They can be found all the way to southern Iceland and from Norway to the polar circle and beyond. Red gurnard (Trigla lucerna), related to the grey gurnard, are not distributed quite so far northward and are entirely absent from the Baltic.

Grey gurnard inhabit depths of about 150 m, preferably in places with a sandy sea bed. However, rocky ground, mud or a mixed floor are also areas where they are to be found. And in the summer months, grey gurnard move to shallow coastal waters at a depth of about 10 m. As a rule, grey gurnard spend their time in groups on the sea bottom; they only venture into more open waters at night, becoming really active with the fall of dusk.

The name "grey gurnard" does not refer to the appearance of the fish, but rather is due to the fact that it makes grunting sounds. They do this by means of special muscles, which cause the swim bladder to vibrate. That is not their only unique characteristic, because they also have the unique ability to "run" along the seabed. This is made possible by free-moving rays in their pelvic fins.

Grey gurnard reproduce between April and August; in the northern

Grey Gurnard

Atlantic this happens as early as February. Females lay 200,000 to 300,000 eggs in open water. The eggs measure 3 to 4 mm in diameter. Fry hatch after approximately seven days. Initially, the young fish live in open waters and eat plankton; they do not switch to the typical lifestyle of a bottom-feeder until they grow to be approximately 3 cm in length.

A maximum length of about 50 cm and weight of 1.5 kg are to be expected for grey gurnard. Average specimens are 25 to 30 cm long and weigh just 400 g.

May to September is the most favourable time for catching grey gurnard; and dusk or bad weather—above all, dim light conditions—have been determined to be especially conducive to success.

Red gurnard look very similar to their grey relations.

Characteristics

Grey gurnards are mostly grey-brown in colour, but there is some variation. They have a rough linear line, because their scales in this area are not only larger than those on the rest of its body, but also have a toothed rear edge and a barbed central spine. The scales at the base of the dorsal fin are also rough. The first dorsal fin is shorter and much higher than the second one; in addition, the first dorsal fin has hard rays, while the second has soft rays. The head of the grey gurnard is armour-plated. The lowest of the three pectoral fin rays is thickened, separated from the remaining fins and free-moving. Laying the pectoral fin flat, it would barely reach the beginning of the anal fin.

Before you try to outwit grey gurnard by legering, prepare your selected fishing spot ahead of time by feeding with fish waste. Light tackle is completely sufficient for this purpose; the bait should be offered on the sea bottom. Take care when landing grey gurnard, because its long, sharp spiny rays can easily cause an injury.

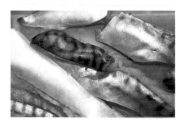

Small chunks of baitfish always meet with good results.

The best bait

Small fish, crabs, worms and shrimp are the natural food sources for grey gurnard. When fishing, therefore, bait such as mudworms, pieces of fish (especially herring and mackerel) as well as shrimp have proven to be particularly successful when angling for grey gurnard.

Peeled shrimps are baited on a single hook.

Cod

Distribution

Cod are found throughout the entire north Atlantic, the Bay of Biscay and in the North Sea. They are absent from the Mediterranean and seldom appear in the eastern part of the Baltic. Their distribution extends as far north as the White Sea.

Cod fishing can be very successful from the shore, too.

There are different species of cod, which can be distinguished from one another according to their rate of growth, distribution and behaviour during reproduction. Generally speaking, cod usually inhabit areas near the sea bottom in coastal waters. Only out at sea are they found from time to time in open waters, far away from the bottom. In order to feel comfortable, they require a water temperature between 2 and 10 °C (36 to 50 °F). During the day the fish come together to form schools in deep water. At dusk, they search out shallower bodies of water in order to feed there. The older cod become, the more ravenously they feed. They have also been known to prey on the young of their own species.

Cod usually spawn between January and April in sufficiently oxygenated bodies of water with a temperature of around 5 °C (41 °F). Cod are extraordinarily productive and the females can produce as many as 9 million eggs, which are 1.5 mm in diameter. The number of eggs is dependent upon the body weight of the female fish. It only takes a few hours for the eggs to rise to the surface; here the fry hatch within two to four weeks. The exact timing depends on the water temperature.

When they have grown to a length of 3 to 6 cm young cod leave open waters and head for the sea bottom. Depending upon the species and environment, this means that they will either seek out very deep areas or shallow water zones.

Cod

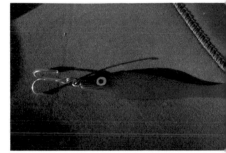

The red pirk is a standard bait for cod.

The best bait

The natural diet of the cod includes crayfish, worms and molluscs of all kinds, so when you are angling for them a good choice of bait is chunks of baitfish or mud-worms. Alternatively, pirks and shrimp have proven to be effective.

Cod grow to an average size of 40 to 60 cm; however they can reach a length of as much as 160 cm and a weight of 45 kg.

The best time to fish for cod is from September to December; however, this can fluctuate depending upon the region and species. Use stable boat or surf-rods equipped with heavy reels. A heavy line is also a necessity in order to angle successfully. Good places to fish are drop offs, reefs, shipwrecks or basically any area with a stony or rocky mixed bottom. Present the bait close to the sea bottom.

Characteristics

The colouration of the cod depends upon its environment and varies anywhere from a reddish or greenish to a pale grey. They have a yellowish-red marbled-effect and yellowish-red spots, and the lateral line is noticeably light. The upper jaw is longer than the lower jaw and protrudes somewhat; the snout is longer than the diameter of the eye. The substantial barbels on its chin and the smooth scales are further distinctive characteristics of the cod. They have three large dorsal and two anal fins.

Hand-length artificial cuttlefish are mounted on a side leader and employed as accompanying bait.

Halibut

DE: Heilbutt,
FR: Flétan,
ES: Fletán,
NL: Heilbot,
SE: Hälleflundra,
helgeflundra,
PL: Halibut biały

Distribution

Halibut mainly inhabit the region around the polar circle. They are to be found from north Norway and Iceland to the Orkney Islands and the Scottish coast. Additionally, they are found from the west of Ireland to the Bay of Biscay.

These flatfish, almost without exception, live at the bottom of the sea. They are rather undemanding, willing to live on both hard and soft area of the sea floor. Now and then, they do venture out into open waters. No matter where the predatory halibut are found, they are an active ocean inhabitant, found at depths of up to 1,000 m. They are most often located somewhere around 300 m below the water surface; only a few prime specimens dare to go into shallow sections of water.

The most important spawning grounds for halibut lie along the southern escarpment of the undersea ridge that runs between Scotland and Greenland, off Newfoundland and the Norwegian coast. The fish reproduce between December and April. They look for deep bodies of water, where the female lays up to 3.5 million eggs, approximately 4 mm in size, near the bottom. These remain in deep water until the fry hatch about two weeks later. After their transformation, the young fish spend their early years at a maximum depth of 100 m, already living the typical life of a bottom-feeder. As they grow older they withdraw into still deeper waters.

Halibut can grow to 3 to 4 m in length and tip the scales at 300 kg; their average size, though, is between 150 and 200 cm. The male fish most often remain smaller than the females. Because these flatfish grow very slowly, it is not unusual for them to be around 30 years of age when they reach their full size.

The best time to catch halibut is from March to October, though this

Characteristics

The body of these right-eyed flatfish is trim and stretched-out; most often it is a single colour, dark brown or black. The starting point of the dorsal fin is above the upper eye; the long mouth opening ends under the lower eye. Above the pelvic fin, the lateral line describes a curve; the background of the front gill cover is open and easy to recognise. The lower jaw of this smooth-scaled fish is longer than the upper jaw.

Halibut

Rubber fish of 25 cm and more in length can be used when angling for halibut.

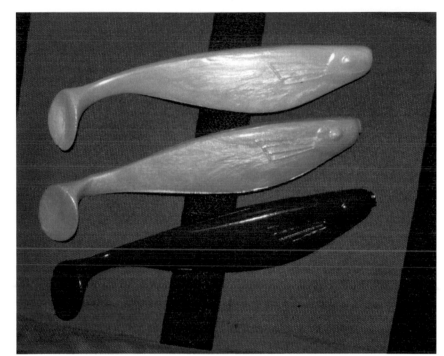

varies somewhat regionally. As a rule, the months of March, April and September have proven to be particularly good for catching halibut. For angling such giant fish you need a heavy boat rod and a multiplier reel spooled with stronger braided line. A gaff is of enormous value when landing halibut. The bait should be presented at various depths in the region from the sea-bed to approximately 20 m above it. Halibut fishing requires great patience, but when the fish finally do bite, the reward is a prime fish.

The underside of this flatfish is quite light.

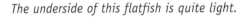

The best bait

The halibut's natural food sources consist of deep-sea shrimp, bullheads, sand eels, herring, cod (Gadus morhua), cuttlefish, cephalopods and different kinds of crustacea.

Above all, whole mackerel and pieces of fish are effective as bait. Large rubber fish can work well as an accompanying bait, mounted on a side leader.

Push large, sharp single hooks through the back of the rubber fish.

Whiting

DE: Wittling,
ES: Merlán,
FR: Lécaud, merlan,
NL: Wijting,
SE: Vitling,
PL: Witlinek

Distribution

Whiting are found in the north Atlantic region from the Bay of Biscay over the North Sea up to about the middle of the Norwegian coast. Their range includes the Icelandic coast, the south-east of the British Isles and the western part of the Baltic. A subspecies lives in the south, in the area of the Iberian Peninsula and in the Mediterranean Sea.

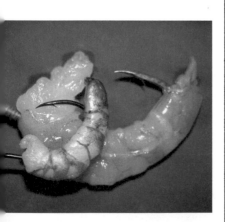

Whiting dine happily on such tasty shrimp morsels.

Whiting live near the bottom at depths of around 200 m and prefer a muddy or gravelly sea bottom, though they also feel very comfortable where the seabed is sand or rock. They are also often found near deep reefs or large solid structures such as piers, breakwaters or causeways. They like to form large shoals. Whiting will hunt near the surface when shoals of the fish on which they prey are swimming there. Turbulent water does not agree with them, and so in rough seas they are even more likely to withdraw to extremely deep waters.

Whiting reproduce during April and May. Depending upon their home waters, though, it is possible for these to fish reproduce at times which are spread out over the whole year. The females lay their eggs in open water in areas of 30 to 100 m in depth. The number of eggs depends upon the size of the female and may reach a maximum of 1 million.

The eggs, and later the fry as well, prefer to hide themselves under jellyfish. The young fish are carried by currents over a wide area of open sea, and only switch to a life on the sea bottom after they have grown to be 10 cm long.

Mature whiting reach a length of at most 70 cm and weigh up to a little over 3 kg. Fish of up to 20 years of age have been known.

Whiting

Pieces of mackerel stay on the hook and always catch whiting.

Characteristics

Whiting vary in colour from a yellowish brown to dark blue or green; their flanks are yellowish-grey and the abdomen is silvery-white. Often, they have a small, dark spot on the upper underside of the pectoral fin. Whiting have an extended body and a rather small head with an upper jaw which protrudes. The snout is longer than the diameter of the eye and is filled with relatively long, pointy teeth. While the young animals still have a short chin barbel, this is not present when they reach maturity. The lateral line of the whiting is relatively dark and easy to recognise.

The best bait

Adult whiting feed primarily on fish (for example, cod and herring), and will even eat smaller fish of their own species. They like to refresh themselves with shrimp.

The choice of bait when fishing for whiting is rather extensive. Besides the particularly successful use of baitfish like mackerel and pieces of fish (herring or mackerel), the use of mud worms and pieces of shrimp may lead to splendidly successful catches.

However, such fish are unusual, and an average whiting measures around 35 cm in length on the hook.

As a rule, the best time to catch whiting is between September and January. However, the exact time varies from region to region. Utilise light boat rods and a multiplier reel, though not too large. Also important are a thin leader and, because of the size of the fish and deep-water currents, weights of around 300 g. Present the bait near the sea bottom.

The main thing to remember when using baitfish or fish pieces is that they should be fresh, because whiting will otherwise ignore the bait. Good places to catch them are, for example, over a sandy seabed in bays, as long as they are deep enough. Other spots to catch whiting are above a shipwreck or reef.

Feathered paternoster tackle garnished with fish pieces are an often used bait.

Ling

DE: Leng, FR: Lingue, ES: Maruca, NL: Leng, SE: Långa, PL: Molwa

Distribution

Ling live off the coasts of the north Atlantic, the North Sea and the Mediterranean. They occur around the British Isles to Brittany and further along the Iberian Peninsula to the Mediterranean. Likewise, they can be found in the area of Norway and eastwards into the Kattegat.

Ling prefer rocky sea floors and live, as a rule, at depths of 100 to 400 m on the bottom. They are usually to be found in areas which have good possibilities for cover, for example among shipwrecks or reefs. Ling are very ravenous, predatory fish. Their young grow very quickly, requiring lots of food, and so the

Ling

This ling could not resist a juicy morsel of fish offered by an angler.

young fish are frequently found near the shore, where they hunt for prey in the rocky stretches.

The spawning period for ling begins earliest in the Mediterranean, where it may commence in March and continue until July. The most important spawning grounds for ling lie in the Bay of Biscay and to the west of the British Isles. On average, the depth of water at the spawning grounds is approximately 200 m. Each female produces 20 million to 60 million eggs which are 1 mm in diameter. The exact number of eggs laid depends upon the size of the female.

Young fish start out living in open water, but switch after only a few years to life on the seabed. On average, ling grow to be 60 to 100 cm long and weigh in at approximately 7 kg. Specimens up to a length of 200 cm do occur, though in general the maximum size is 160

Characteristics

The ling is a fish with a very long and trim body; its back is reddish-brown and becomes lighter and lighter over the flanks to the abdomen, which is coloured white. Its chin barbel is longer than the diameter of its eye, and it sports a black spot on the back end of its first dorsal fin. The tale shaft is relatively broad, and its fins have a narrow band of white.

cm in length and 35 kg in weight. Most males remain smaller than the females.

Ling can be caught throughout the year. However, they bite particularly well from the beginning of March to the end of October. In the period from November to February, you only stand a good chance of catching ling if the bait is presented deeply enough, at least 200 m. Good places to catch ling are areas which offer them sufficient possibilities to take cover, for example, steep edges, reefs or wrecks. With stable sea rods and a large multiplier reel equipped with strong, braided line you have a good chance of catching ling. Naturally, present the bait for these bottom-feeders on or just above the seabed. The hooks need to be particularly sharp because the ling's mouth is like leather, which makes it more difficult for the hook to penetrate.

The best bait

The primary source of food for ling consists of other fishes; they prefer whiting, cod, flatfish and grey gurnard. They also eat cephalopods and crayfish.

When choosing bait, give priority to fish. Besides the species which the ling preys upon in its natural environment, the sand eel has also proven to be a good option. Cuttlefish and shrimp may be tried as alternatives. Among artificial baits, pirks catch the most lings.

The feathered paternoster is a standard when fishing for ling.

Short-spined Sea Scorpion

Other names: Greater bull-head, rout, plucker, bull rout, father lasher

DE: Seeskorpion, ES: Coto, FR: Chabot, NL: Zeedonderpad, SE: Ulk, rödsimpa, PL: Kur diabel

Distribution

Short-spined sea scorpions are plentiful in the North and Baltic Seas. In the north Atlantic their range includes waters off the British Isles to the Bay of Biscay. They inhabit the Scandinavian coast and may even be found as far as the White Sea, but are not at home in the Mediterranean.

The short-spined sea scorpion will happily take mussel meat.

Short-spined sea scorpions are found in shallow water up to about 200 m in depth, as long as the water temperature remains between 0 and 15 °C (32 and 59 °F). These bottom-dwelling fish live on rocky ocean floors, as well as on sand or mud bottoms. They prefer underwater vegetation, where they hide amongst stones, seaweed or algae. They are not especially hard to please, as evinced by the fact that they may also be found in brackish waters. Short-spined sea scorpions are ravenous, predatory fish, faithful to their location. There are many different local species.

The short-spined sea scorpions' spawning period extends from January to March, though the timing varies regionally—in some areas the spawning period begins as early as October. The male keeps a firm grip around the female with the

abdominal and pectoral fins during the act. The fertilization of the eggs takes place internally, and the male sea scorpion has a short semen tube for this purpose. Approximately 2,500 eggs up to 2.5 mm in size are then laid in clumps on the sea bottom. Subsequently, the male guards the batch of eggs until the fry hatch about five weeks later. Initially, young short-spined sea scorpions live in open water, switching to life on the sea floor when they have reached a size of about 15 mm.

Short-spined sea scorpions grow to an average length of 20 to 35 cm and a weight of 500 g. Their maximum size is approximately 60 cm in length.

Short-spined Sea Scorpion

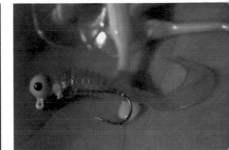

When spin fishing with light tackle, pursue this glutton with small twisters.

The best bait

The short-spined sea scorpion feeds on small fish, crayfish and snails; however, it is something of an omnivore; therefore, there is no single really any outstanding bait. Small spinners have proven themselves, as have baitfish, pieces of fish, shrimp and mussel meat. Basically, the short-spined sea scorpion will bite when offered any kind of sea bait.

Characteristics

Short-spined sea scorpions have a green-brown coloured back. They often have a dark spot and milky white points on their pelvic fins. The abdomen, normally white, is cherry-red on the males during the spawning season; the females are more likely to have orange-coloured abdomens, also decorated with white points. Short-spined sea scorpions have a mighty head, which is covered with points and barbs, a large mouth and large eyes. All their fins have bands and are spotted; the pectoral fins are very large. The first of its two dorsal fins has spined rays. The gill membranes have grown together under the throat with a diagonal crease; the longest barb on the front gill cover does not reach the back edge of the gill. Short-spined sea scorpions do not have armour-plated bodies.

Short-spined sea scorpions are not necessarily one of the best-loved fish amongst anglers, because these greedy omnivores are constantly found on the hook when the intended catch was an entirely different fish.

Should you set out to catch the short-spined sea scorpion on purpose, though, the best time is from May to September. Use light tackle with leger rods, or spin or float rods. Areas of water with stones or seaweed are always good places to find this fish, as are harbours or close in to the coast. The bait is presented on or directly above the sea floor. If using spinners as bait, these should be at a considerable depth.

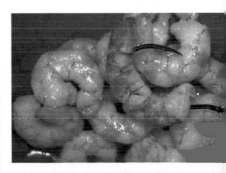

Shrimp is an easily obtainable bait.

Plaice

Other names: Henfish, European plaice, fluke

DE: Scholle, FR: Plie, carrelet, ES: Solla, NL: Schol, SE: Rödspotta, rödspätta, PL: Gladzica

Distribution

Plaice live in the coastal areas of the White Sea down to Gibraltar. They are even to be found in the North Sea as well as in the western part of the Baltic. In the Mediterranean, their range is limited to the area from Gibraltar to Monaco.

Crayfish tails stay on the hook well; therefore, they are particularly well-suited for shore fishing.

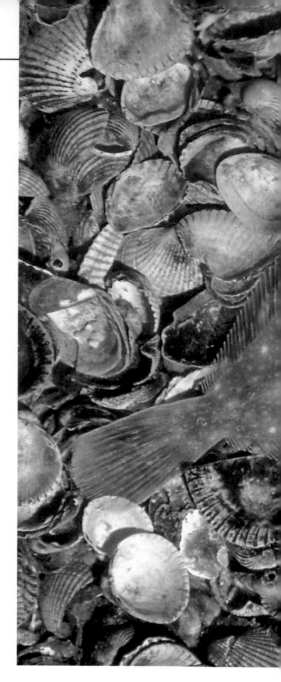

Plaice favour bodies of water with medium to shallow depths; primarily they are to be found at depths between 50 and 70 m. Smaller specimens, however, tend to live not quite as deep as the largest specimens, which may be at depths of up to 150 m. Plaice like sandy or muddy seabeds; therefore, sand bars surrounded by particularly strong currents are some of their preferred environments. Plaice roam around in schools when they go searching for prey as dusk falls. During the day, they are only really active when the weather is wet, cold and overcast. On very warm and sunny days, plaice would far rather bury themselves and wait for the evening hours.

Plaice reproduce at water temperatures around 6 °C (43 °F) at a depth of 20 to 40 m; therefore, the spawning times vary regionally. In the North Sea, for example, reproduction takes place between January and April, while the plaice in the

Barents Sea only spawn from March to May. Depending upon the size of the female, between 50,000 to 500,000 eggs of 1.6 mm will be released in open water. These eggs require a rather high concentration of salt in the water to be able to drift in the open; otherwise they sink to the floor and die.

As soon as the fry switch to actively taking in food, they become very sensitive to, among other things, a lack of food. Continuous periods of cold also constitute a danger, because this retards their

Plaice

The best bait

The natural diet of the plaice consists of bristle worms, crayfish and mussels. When selecting your bait, mussel meat should be given preference; sand worms or crayfish are other good options.

Plaice can seldom resist a bit of mussel on a hook.

growth, delaying their development into young fish.

Exceptional plaice may grow to lengths of 90 cm and weigh up to 6 kg; however specimens between 30 and 40 cm and weighing 500 g are more common.

From May to September is the time to catch plaice, and the best opportunities are at night. If you are going to fish during the day wait for a day when the weather is rather poor to improve your chances. Use light boat rods or long surf rods. The reels should not be too large, nor the lines too thick. Particularly good places to catch plaice are sand bars where sand eels can be found.

Characteristics

This right-eyed flatfish is grey-brown or green-brown coloured on the upper side and covered with irregular orange-coloured to red spots; the abdomen is white. The lateral line is relatively straight and does not describe an actual curve above the pelvic fin. Plaice have a small mouth and the dorsal fin extends to its upper eye.

They are often confused with flounder. However, the plaice have extremely smooth skin, while that of the flounder is rather rough.

Pollack

Distribution

Pollack inhabit the coastal waters of the Atlantic from the north of Norway to the British Isles, including Ireland, all the way to Morocco. They are also found in the North Sea.

Pollack like to live near the sea bottom and also in open water; they can be found near the coast as well as at a depth of up to 200 m. They prefer a rocky bottom that offers possibilities for taking cover, for example, reefs and shipwrecks; however, they will sometimes also choose to live near oil platforms. Young fish often form shoals with similar-sized coalfish. While mature adults still appear mostly in groups, they have cast aside their shoal-building behaviour.

Pollacks spawn in the spring and reproduce near the coast in areas with a depth of 100 to 200 m. The eggs drift in open water, as do the fry, which hatch after seven days. The young fish live in open water as well and spend their time near the coast before they take up the lifestyle of the adults two to three years later.

An average pollack weighs 600 g to 2 kg and is 40 to 60 cm long. These fish can become 130 cm long at a maximum and tip the scales at approximately 10 kg, however, they seldom reach more than 100 cm.

Pollack bite particularly well between July and September, but they can be caught outside this time period, provided you know where to look. From March to May, they spend their time primarily near the bottom,

Pollack

Characteristics

The dark colouration of the back of the pollack turns into a yellowish-green on the flanks, then changes abruptly to the silver-white to grey colour of the abdomen. Fish of this species have a trim body and a projecting, extended lower jaw without a chin barbel. The lateral line is rather dark and runs in an arch above the pelvic fin. Except for the light, yellowish pelvic fins, the fins of the pollack are darkly coloured.

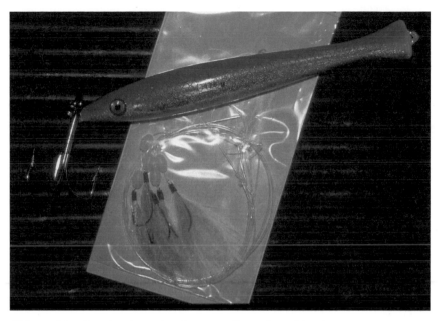

Pirks and feathered paternoster rigs—an oft-used combination.

before they go into open waters in search of prey well into September. As soon as the weather becomes colder, they withdraw again into deeper water levels. If you take this into consideration, you can target this fish with much success. Good places to catch them are, for example, ledges, reefs or harbour holes, as long as these extend into deep water levels.

You can fish either from a boat with light boat rods or spin fishes from the bank with strong tackle. A medium-heavy float rod is another possibility to outwit the pollack. In any case, the rods should not be too large and should be spooled with medium-strength line. The bait is presented between the bottom and medium-deep water, depending upon the time of the year and your preferred fishing method. Pollack bites are customarily strong and unambiguous, and the fish tend to flee with intensity.

The best bait

In its natural environment the primary elements of the pollacks' diet are herring and crayfish. Among artificial baits, the paternoster system with feathers and a pirk have proven to make outstanding bait. However, the jumping imitations of sand eels or shrimp, as well as twisters, likewise promise success.

Twisters of about 15 cm in length are a good choice for the pollack.

A catch like this one is a real thrill.

Coalfish

Other names: Saithe, coley
DE: Köhler, Seelachs
F: Lieu noir, ES: Carbonero,
NL: Koolvis, SE: Sej, gråsej,
PL: Czarniak

Distribution

Coalfish are distributed along the coast of the north Atlantic. You come across it around Iceland as well as the British Isles and the Bay of Biscay. Likewise, coalfish are found in the North Sea and occasionally in the Baltic. Generally, they avoid bodies of water which have a low salt content, for example the central Baltic Sea.

Trim, shiny pirks attract the coalfish at greater depths.

The best bait

As fully mature fish, adult coalfish eat glow-shrimp, herring, young cod, sprat and even the young of their own species.

Small fish of the species mentioned above or pieces of fish make outstanding bait. You can also achieve success with small, trim pirks, rubber fish, streamers or the paternoster system.

Coalfish are an open water fish and can be found in an extremely wide range of depths, from the surface to approximately 250 m. In early spring they make their way closer to the coast and shallower waters. In winter they withdraw into deeper waters further out to sea. In contrast to their relative the pollack, coalfish not only form shoals when they are young, but remain decidedly social as adults. They like to spend time near wrecks or even oil platforms. Coalfish are some of the fastest and most elegant representatives of the cod family. While searching for food, they range widely within their distribution area. They will happily chase after shoals of herring, following the herrings' course as they rise up to the surface and descend again.

Coalfish begin their spawning season in January, and it lasts into April. At a water temperature of 6 to 8 °C (43 to 46 °F), the fish head for spawning waters north of the British Isles and off the coast of Norway. One of the characteristics of the spawning areas favoured by the coalfish is a high salt concentration. Here, the eggs are laid at a depth of approximately 200 m.

Young coalfish spend the first two to three years of their lives in large shoals in coastal waters. These long-lived fish can reach the age of 30 years and record weights of 20 kg. Specimens of 130 cm have been known; however, the average is more like 60 to 80 cm and 5 kg in weight.

Use rubber fish as an additional bait on a side leader, or as the only bait when spin fishing.

Coalfish

Characteristics

Coalfish have a brownish-green back which becomes brighter at the flanks, but not as strongly green-yellowish as the pollack. The rest of the flank and the sides of the abdomen are likewise silver-grey and white.

Adults have a projecting and extended lower jaw and no chin barbel. However, young coalfish still have a small chin barbel. Coalfish have a straight lateral line in light relief. The pelvic fins are very light; the other fins are all very dark.

The best fishing season for coalfish begins in July and lasts until September. Then, in addition to their typical haunts, coalfish are often to be found in strong currents. If you are boat fishing, light rods rigged with paternoster tackle (i. e. short leaders with hook appended to the main line, with the weight fixed at the extreme end) is a system that brings good results. When fishing further out to sea, however, use stable tackle, because this is where the largest coalfish lurk. Reels and lines should not be too large or coarse in either case.

If you prefer solid ground under your feet you can still achieve successful coalfish catches from the shore using medium spin rods and introducing the bait quickly. Coalfish tend to flee rapidly, which is why the drag control should be adjusted very finely.

Blue Shark

Other names:
Great blue shark

DE: Bluahai, FR: Peau bleu,
requin bleu, empereur,
ES: Tintorera, NL: Blauwe
haai, SE: Blåhaj,
PL: arłacz błękitny

Distribution

*Blue sharks have a range
that extends from the
coasts of the Mediterranean
to the Iberian Peninsula,
from west of the British
Isles to south-east of Norway. However, they only venture into the cooler regions
during the summertime,
which is also when they
turn up in the North Sea.*

Characteristics

*The blue shark gets its
name from the dark blue
colouration of its back. The
flanks are also blue,
although lighter; the abdomen is white. Blue sharks
can be recognised by their
long, pointy snout, large
eyes and the long, sickle-
shaped pectoral fin. The
mouth is full of triangular
teeth which are equipped
with fine saw-like edges on
both sides.*

Blue sharks live in the open waters of the ocean; however, they also appear in large numbers near the coast. As a rule they are to be found in deep bodies of water—at least 150 m—where they can cover great distances when pursuing shoals of fish. Often, blue sharks swim near the surface so that their back and caudal fins project out of the water.

Blue sharks are viviparous (live-bearing) and reach sexual maturity at four or five years old. Female blue sharks are able to mate even earlier and to save the sperm. In this case, when the female reaches sexual maturity the first mature egg cells are fertilized by the female blue shark herself, in a manner of speaking. As a rule however, the male shark holds onto his partner firmly during mating. This has never been directly observed, but clear bite marks on the skin of the female (which is three times thicker the male's skin) testifies to blue sharks' behaviour being akin to that of other species of shark.

The embryos are nourished in the mother's body through a placenta; gestation lasts 9 to 12 months. On

Blue Shark

A plump mackerel is always a good choice of bait for the blue shark.

average females bear 25 to 50 young at a go, between 40 and 50 cm long, though the number of young born at one time can range anywhere from four to as many as 135. The number seems to depend upon the size of the mother.

Blue sharks may reach lengths of up to 4 m long and weigh 200 kg, though you rarely catch a glimpse of such exceptional specimens, but are more likely to encounter animals weighing about 30 kg.

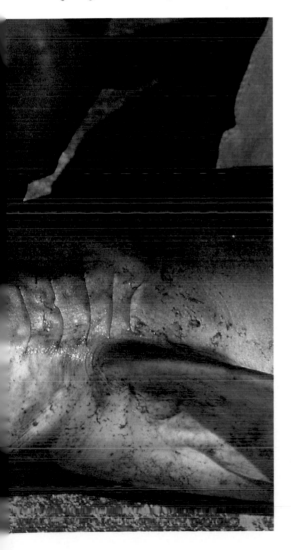

The best bait

Blue sharks feed primarily on shoal fish including mackerel and herring, though squid also form part of their natural diet. When angling for them, try baiting with mackerel and herring, whole or in pieces, or with cuttlefish.

Blue sharks can be caught all year round. The first step is to catch suitable baitfish such as mackerel. When the bait is ready and you are all prepared to hunt these big-game fish, you will need sturdy equipment. Large floats, medium to heavy boat rods, as well as a large multiplier reel with braided line are just as necessary as sharp hooks and a steel leader. The strength of the rods and your tackle is altogether dependent on the size of the shark you expect to catch—when in doubt, make inquiries on site beforehand. In order to entice blue sharks, feed them with bait and discarded fish ahead of time.

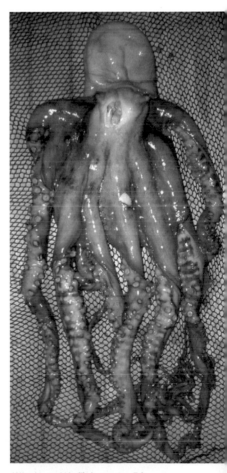

Whole cuttlefish up to 50 cm long are employed as bait.

Turbot

Other names: Breet, britt
DE: Steinbutt, FR: Turbot,
ES: Rodaballo, NL: Tarbot,
SE: Piggvar, PL: Turbot

Distribution

Turbot occur in northern Atlantic waters ranging from the coasts of the British Isles to waters south and west of Norway, the south of Sweden and Denmark. They are also found all around the Iberian Peninsula and in the entire Mediterranean region as far as the Black Sea.

Pieces of fish, like the sardines pictured here, are baited on single hooks.

The best bait

Turbot predominantly feed on bottom-dwelling fish (for example, sand eel), but they will also take mussels and large crayfish.

When making your selection of bait, try baitfish and fish pieces at first. In addition to sand eel, mackerel and herring have proven to be extremely effective at luring turbot. Alternatively, give crayfish or mussels a try.

Turbot are found where the sea bottom is stony, sandy or of mixed media. Here they live at depths of 20 to 70 m. They favour bodies of water where an even bottom is suddenly interrupted by irregularities such as gullies or reef edges. Flatfish like turbot, true to their habitat, tend not to travel far when searching for food, but rather wait within reach, so to speak, in their preferred environment. Those turbot which are found in shallower water are usually young fish; older specimens are more frequently found in deep water.

The spawning season for turbot is between April and August. The females lay between 5 million and 15 million eggs, with a diameter of approximately 1 mm, in water 15 to 40 m deep. It takes between seven and nine days until the fry hatch. At first, the young fish live in open water, switching to life on the sea bottom when they reach a length of about 25 mm.

Generally, female turbot grow faster than the male and they grow larger, too. The average length of a male amounts to only 35 cm, while females average 45 cm. The maximum recorded length for a turbot is 100 cm, with a maximum weight of 25 kg. Specimens of over 50 cm (male) or 79 cm (female) are very rare.

The best time to catch turbot is from June to September. Strong boat rods and long surf rods with a medium fixed-spool reel or a multiplier reel are necessary, as are strong lines. When choosing a location, consider areas where the sea floor suddenly changes and where there are obstacles, for example sand bars or wrecks. Slowly lower the bait when trolling and direct the bait with sensitivity. Generally, it is best to present the bait directly above the sea bottom.

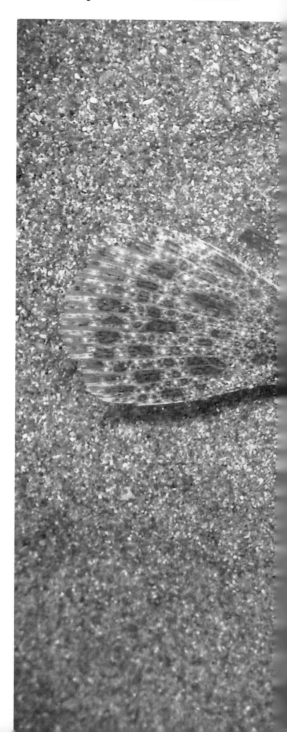

Turbot

If turbot bite successfully, do not take up the fight immediately, because they usually do not swallow the bait at once. A gaff is very helpful for landing the fish; in case there is none within reach, make absolutely sure you have included a large landing net with your equipment.

Small, whole mullet can be used as bait.

Characteristics

These left-eyed, dark flat-fish have a nearly circular body and an eye-side without scales, but which is full of bone tuberosity. Their shape and colour allow them to blend in with their surroundings. The starting point of the dorsal fin lies above the upper eye; the lateral line describes an arch above the pectoral fin.

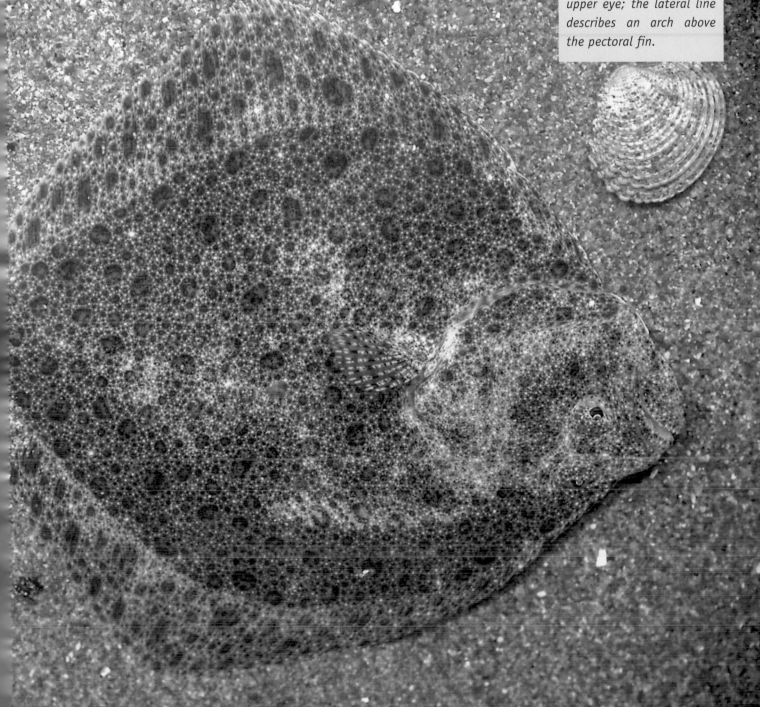

Thornback Ray

Other names: Maiden ray, roker, thornback rough ray, thornback maid ray, thornback skate, thorny

DE: Nagelrochen, FR: Raie bouclée, ES: Raya de clavos, NL: Stekelrog, SE: Knaggrocka, PL: Raja nabijana, Raja ciernista

Distribution

The thornback ray is at home from the Mediterranean region including the Black Sea to the Atlantic, and from the North Sea to the Baltic. You find them off the Iberian coast, around the British Isles, south-west Norway, the south of Sweden and Denmark and likewise off the coast of Iceland.

Giant shrimp, threaded onto the hook whole, are an outstanding bait.

Thornback rays are the most common type of ray in Europe and prefer to live in soft, sandy to muddy ocean floors. They are most often found at depths of 20 to 100 m; however, they at times withdraw to regions up to 300 m deep. As a rule, thornback rays prefer shallow water zones, even river estuaries. Because their five gill folds are to be found on the underside of the body, these rays have a so-called spray-hole under each eye, which directs the "breathing water" to the gills whenever they lie on the sea bottom. Without this adaptation, they would breath in sand or mud. When swimming, thornback rays breathe completely normally through their gills.

Thornback Ray

Characteristics

The thornback ray's back is coloured in various dark brown tones, mottled with numerous dark and light yellow-grey spots. There are patches of rough spikes (the thorns) along the back and, on larger specimens, bigger spikes on and under the wings. The underside is white. Thornback rays have a short snout and sharp wing ends on a rhombic body disc. The light tail is distinctly separate from the body and is equipped with dark, diagonal bands.

A few weeks later the female begins to lay one square egg capsule daily. In total, every year a female lays up to 150 egg capsules. These have horn-like extensions at their ends which provide the embryo with breathing water. After four to five months, the young rays hatch, measuring about 12 cm long.

Female rays may grow to a maximum length of 120 cm and weigh up to 18 kg. Males remain smaller and, at 70 cm, reach just about half the size of the female.

The most favourable time to fish for rays is from July to October. You need strong tackle and should therefore choose a very stable boat rod. You will need large reels outfitted with strong line; in addition, it is necessary to use a steel leader. Present the bait directly on the bottom. Good places to fish are relatively shallow areas with a muddy or sandy bottom. If you choose a fishing spot where crayfish are numerous, the thornback ray should not be far away.

Thornback rays are angled from boats with a multiplier reel and braided line.

The best bait

Thornback rays prefer to feed on crustacea of all kinds: they will take crabs, shrimp, small fish and mussels. Take this into consideration when choosing your bait, and use shrimp and crabs as first choice where available.

You could alternatively use mussel meat or fist-sized pieces of fish—mackerel has proven to be a particularly successful bait.

Thornback rays generally reproduce in the springtime; in the Mediterranean region, however, reproduction may also take place in the wintertime. By means of a stick-like copulation organ on the inner edge of its pelvic fin, the male clamps himself firmly on the female ray, and internal fertilization takes place.

Mackerel

Other names: Atlantic mackerel, Joey

DE: Makrele,
FR: Maquereau, ES: Caballa del Atlántico, NL: Makreel, paapje, SE: Makrill,
PL: Makrela

Distribution

Mackerel live in the north-eastern Atlantic, in the Bay of Biscay, and from the Mediterranean to the Black Sea. Its area of distribution also includes the North Sea and the Baltic.

The paternoster is absolutely the best way to catch mackerel when fishing from a cutter.

Mackerel are shoal fish which undertake far-reaching treks, and largely live in open water near the surface. During the winter, however, the shoals are to be found near the ocean floor and do not eat at all. Only at the beginning of spring do they begin to feed again, limiting themselves at first to the smallest sea creatures as food. Simultaneously, they begin their ascent into warmer zones again, where they spend their time at the surface, preferably somewhere near a coast.

With the mackerel of the north-eastern Atlantic a differentiation is made between the eastern and the western stock, and their spawning periods differ from one another. Taken as a whole, their reproductive period lasts from May to July, with the western mackerel spawning somewhat earlier. Mackerel from the Mediterranean region reproduce as early as March and April.

The females produce between 200,000 and 450,000 eggs near the water surface, releasing them in open water. Mackerel eggs measure 0.9 to 1.4 mm; the fry hatch after

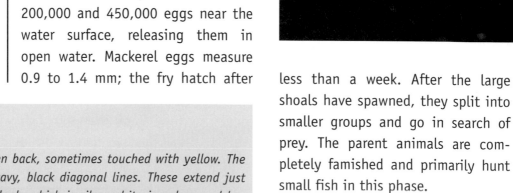

less than a week. After the large shoals have spawned, they split into smaller groups and go in search of prey. The parent animals are completely famished and primarily hunt small fish in this phase.

An average mackerel is up to 30 cm long and tips the scale at nearly 1 kg. The maximum weight for mackerel is 2.5 kg, and the greatest length is 60 cm.

Characteristics

Mackerel have a glowing green back, sometimes touched with yellow. The back is marked with many wavy, black diagonal lines. These extend just about to the middle of the flank, which is silver-white in colour and has a mother-of-pearl type glint to it, exactly like the abdomen. Behind the anal fin and the two dorsal fins, the mackerel has five small fins on the tail shaft. The tail fin almost always has sickle-shaped notches.

Mackerel

The best bait

Mackerel feed on animal plankton and fish spawn, but they also eat the smallest crayfish and molluscs, as well as small fish.

A paternoster rig with feathers has proven to be an outstanding means to catch mackerel. Alternatively, employ small spinners and pieces of baitfish.

The best opportunity to go fishing for mackerel is after they have spawned. Obviously this will depend on where you are fishing: the optimum time period starts in August in the east, in July in the west, or begins as early as May in the Mediterranean.

Light to medium boat rods suffice when fishing with a paternoster rig; however, they need to be long boat rods. Small multiplier reels or medium fixed-spool reels, both equipped with strong line, are suitable. Strong line is also useful when spin fishing with light tackle. Present the bait near the surface unless you are fishing outside of the main fishing season, in which case you can go down to about 200 m.

With a colourful spinner on a light rod, mackerel fishing becomes a successful adventure.

Redfish

Other names:
Rosefish

DE: Rotbarsch, FR: Grand
sébaste, ES: Gallineta
dorada, NL: Roodbaars,
SE: Rödfisk, kungsfisk,
PL: Karmazyn atlantycki

Distribution

*The redfish is a fish of the
northern oceans. Their area
of distribution includes the
north Atlantic and the
North Sea from Iceland to
the Orkney Islands and the
coast of Norway.*

Redfish have been fished com-
mercially for more than half a
century already, but there is not
much known about its biology. Great
redfish primarily live in depths
between 100 and 1,000 m and far
away from the coast. Young redfish
spend their time in bays, fjords or
near the coast. Generally, there is a
greater likelihood of finding the
related species, the lesser redfish
(*Sebastes viviparus*). The great
redfish mostly live on the sea
bottom near undersea shelves, for
example. However, they also appear
in the open sea. As a rule, these

gregarious fish are more likely to be
found in shallow water at night, if
at all. During the day they keep to
far deeper water.

Redfish are viviparous (live-
bearing) and mate between late
summer and the autumn. Because
the eggs are not at all mature by
this time, the female saves the
semen in her body well into the
winter; only then are the mature
eggs fertilized. After mating successfully, female redfish migrate to
the spawning locations. Up to
350,000 fry, approximately 8 mm in
length, are born. The exact number

Redfish

If the redfish are located in deep water, a pirk is the bait to use.

Rubber fish are a tempting bait for the redfish.

of offspring a female redfish produces depends upon her size. The young redfish live in open water near the surface until they grow to be 4 cm. Then they relocate down to depths of 100 to 200 m.

Redfish grow very slowly, and only take on their red colouration when they reach an average size of circa 15 cm, by which time they are already about four years old. An average adult redfish grows to 40 cm long. Nowadays, redfish over 50 cm in length have become rather rare. Redfish can become twice as large and weigh up to 15 kg, but then they do live a long time and can reach an age of over 60 years.

Characteristics

Redfish have a body that is conspicuously red-gold coloured, tending to more of a silver-white from the pectoral fin onwards. They do not have dark, diagonal bands like the lesser redfish (Sebastes viviparus), and both spikes on the edges of the front gill cover are directed at an upwards or forwards angle. The first three rays of the anal fin are strong spikes; the hard and soft rays of the dorsal fin have grown together.

Fishing for redfish promises success throughout the year, as long as you go far enough out to sea. There, find suitable plateaus starting at a depth of 130 m, where the redfish are to be found, most often in shoals shaped like bunches of grapes. Make sure your equipment includes boat rods and large multiplier reels, in order to be able to start fishing at a depth of 250 m, because this kind of depth requires heavy weights.

The best bait

The diet of the redfish ranges from crayfish in open water to shrimp and fish spawn and even other fish. Only the large specimens eat fish, and they are particularly fond of herring or cod.

Redfish can be caught with artificial bait as well as with natural bait. Next to rubber fish, twisters and small pirks the rubber fish has proven itself particularly efficaceous. It is used as an accompaniment to natural bait (baitfish pieces) and fastened onto a side leader.

Do not disregard rubber bait, like these imitation crabs, as an alternative.

Piked Dogfish

Other names: Spotted spiny dogfish, spur dogfish, blue dog, Darwen salmon, spring dogfish, common spiny fish

DE: Dornhai, FR: Aiguillat, ES: Mielga, NL: Doornhaai, SE: Pigghaj, PL: Kole

Distribution

Piked dogfish occur along the Mediterranean coast and into the Black Sea. In the north Atlantic they are found from the Iberian Peninsula to Iceland. You may also run into them in the North Sea off the British Isles and along the Norwegian coast.

With a single hook in the neck, the eel is used as bait.

Piked dogfish are possibly the most common type of shark; or at least one of the most widely occurring world-wide. Piked dogfish are bottom-feeders and prefer a soft bottom at depths of 10 to 200 m; however, now and then you may even come across specimens at 900 m. Piked dogfish feel most comfortable when the water temperature is between 6 and 15 °C (43–59 °F).

These sharks often congregate in large schools consisting of piked dogfish of one sex and similar-sized individuals. Only rarely do they mingle in mixed schools. Loners occasionally depart and socialize with other species, such as the leopard shark or the brown smooth shark. Piked dogfish travel great distances daily in search of food.

Piked dogfish are viviparous (live-bearing). At the beginning of the 18 to 22-month gestation period, up to six eggs may still be surrounded by a common egg skin. This subsequently dissolves. The number of young depends upon the size of the mother; on average around five small piked dogfish are born at one time. The maximum number in one brood is 20 young, which are then smaller at birth. The young animals are usually 20 to 33 cm long and grow very slowly.

Piked dogfish reach sexual maturity at 10 to 12 years old. Males are capable of reproducing approximately two years before females. Bearing in mind the long gestation period, as well as the small number

The best bait

Because piked dogfish primarily feed on shoal fish such as herring, mackerel or cod, these fish make the best bait. Additionally, eels and pieces of baitfish (about fist-sized) are highly recommended. Among artificial baits, pirks are best. It is also worth remembering that bottom-dwelling invertebrates are part of their natural diet.

of offsping, its not surprising that the much-fished piked dogfish is an endangered species.

Piked dogfish can grow to a maximum length of 120 cm (females, that is) and 90 cm (males) and weigh up to 9 kg. On average, piked

Characteristics

Piked dogfish have a grey-brown back and flank colouration. The abdomen is dirty-white. On the flanks there are often additionally several white spots. The back edge of the pectoral, pelvic and caudal fins are equipped with a pale, light band. The body is long and extended, the head pointed. There are long, sharp bony spines in front of the dorsal fin.

dogfish reach an age of between 20 and 25 years; the greatest age is around 60 years.

The best time to catch piked dogfish is between May and October. When angling for them your equipment must include medium to heavy boat rods and large multiplier reels; the line should be thick and strong, your hooks large and, above all, extremely sharp.

In shallower bodies of water, at around 30 m, the piked dogfish sometimes bites at wigglers, but generally you will succeed best with natural bait. Present the bait near the sea floor; and bear in mind that you need to use a steel leader.

Small shellfish are also suitable for catching piked dogfish.